YOU
CAN'T
DO AT
THAT
WORK

100 LEGAL MISTAKES THAT MANAGERS
MAKE IN THE WORKPLACE

NATASHA **BOWMAN**

The Workplace Doctor

Performance ReNEW Publishing
P.O. Box 513
New York, NY 10463
www.performance-renew.com

Ordering Information:
Quantity sales. Special discounts are available on quantity purchases by corporations, associations, and others. For details, contact the publisher at the address above.

Printed in the United States of America

You Can't Do That at Work! Natasha Bowman, JD, SPHR - 1st ed.
ISBN-13: 978-0692880661
ISBN-10: 0692880666

This book is dedicated to protecting equal employment opportunity

Table of Contents

Preface

BECOMING THE WORKPLACE DOCTOR

y journey to becoming "The Workplace Doctor" has been long, tedious, and adventurous. It has been filled with excitement, twists, and turns as I navigated through the labyrinth of mid-size and Fortune 500 organizations. The beginning of my journey to become a human resource professional, professor, legal academic, consultant, and international speaker wasn't the ideal situation. I grew up in the 80s in Montgomery, Alabama where my mother worked as a teacher and my father worked as a school principal. In other words, there was no clear path or example for a little girl from Alabama to ever work in corporate America. To be honest, I had no idea what a job in "corporate America" looked like until I was well into my 20s. Growing up in Alabama in the 1980s, to be considered rich and successful meant that you worked as a doctor, lawyer, dentist, school principal, politician, or a banker. In fact, Alabama's only Fortune 500 company to this day is Regions Bank. Although I had never seen a corporate environment, I would soon be on a trajectory of working as a corporate manager for the world's largest private employer.

After completing my undergraduate degree, I worked as a file clerk/back-up receptionist at a mid-sized law firm in Alabama. It was there that my journey to becoming The

Workplace Doctor began. Although I was only a file clerk, I had a big, beautiful office and free health insurance, and I worked around professionals. What a job! But one day I was delivered news that would completely change the path of my career. I was asked to supervise a team of "runners" whose responsibilities were to run errands such as picking up lunches for the attorneys, filing documents at the courthouses, and making post office runs. They were all in college and mostly the sons and daughters of the attorneys or their friends' kids. But what made this new role even more challenging was the fact that they were just a little younger than me. These were the kids who I had been joking around with on a day-to-day basis, and now I would be their boss! Not surprisingly, they had the same reaction. "She's going to be our boss?!"

I got to experience firsthand what it was like to be promoted into a supervisory/management position without any training. The terms performance management, employee engagement, and employment law were all new to me. I had no confidence. I felt intimidated that my subordinates were the kids of my bosses and I was absolutely mortified when it came to things like making tough decisions, denying time off, and having difficult conversations when a runner went missing for several hours during the day. To make the best of this role (and to save my job), I knew I needed to do something and do it quickly!

While working at the law firm, I also worked at a department store at night and on the weekends and knew that the human resources manager there was the person who was responsible for handling the matters that I was now handling. So, I decided that nothing would prepare me better for my new position than to enroll in the Human Resources Management graduate program at a university down the street from the law office where I worked. Not only would I learn how to manage day-to-day employee issues, but I would also get a graduate degree that would ultimately lead to a career. We didn't have a human resources department at the law office so I set a goal. After completing my master's degree, I planned to pitch to the managing attorney that I could be the human resources manager for the office of over 200 employees.

To be honest, my first few classes in the master's program were quite boring. They were taught by PhDs who had little or no practical experience to share and we learned mostly theory. I passed with flying colors simply by memorizing the text, but I wasn't being truly nurtured to become an HR professional. Sadly, I was beginning to doubt my choice and had second thoughts about completing the degree until I enrolled in an employment law class. It was taught by an HR Director who was also an employment law attorney. I could not get enough of that class and of hearing the stories she would share about her HR experiences (of workplace bullying, discrimination, sexual harassment, and FMLA violations) in the workplace. At that moment, I knew exactly what I wanted to be when I grew up! A lawyer, an HR professional, and a professor. I wanted to be just like her.

I immediately began to study for the law school admittance test (LSAT) to begin my journey. I did quite well and earned a scholarship to the University of Arkansas Law School in Fayetteville, Arkansas, which just so happened to be just a couple of towns over from Bentonville, Arkansas, where the home office of Walmart Stores, Inc. is located. Although I had been offered many scholarships to from different law schools, Walmart's close proximity to the University of Arkansas was one of the primary reasons I chose this as my destination.

I was certain I wanted to utilize my law degree to enhance my HR credentials and I knew I wanted to be in HR for the largest private employer in the world. During my second year of law school, I was presented with that opportunity by way of a corporate externship program between the University of Arkansas and Walmart. I was able to work in the legal department and receive credit while working towards my law degree. At the completion of my externship, I was offered a paid internship in the legal department. Eventually, I went to work as a law clerk for the country's largest labor and employment law firm. This was a key move because that law firm served as one of Walmart's outside legal councils, which afforded me the opportunity to continue to work on Walmart's legal cases.

Upon graduation from law school, I went back to work for Walmart in a newly formed employment compliance group that was established to address the many allegations of discrimination, working off the clock, union mitigation, and other employment compliance issues that Walmart was facing at that time. There could not have been a better opportunity for a new and budding HR professional with a legal background like myself. At that time, Walmart was facing legal problems for almost anything and everything that any organization could be sued for as it related to labor and employment law. I was fortunate to be there developing solutions by participating in and leading efforts to: rewrite policies; provide subject matter expertise to the development of a new time and attendance system that were programs for compliance according to each state's wage and hour laws; develop processes for disability accommodation requests; roll out diversity initiatives; and much, much more. To work in a department like this at Walmart, not only did you have to be an expert at the federal level of labor and employment law, but you also had to know the intricacies of state and local labor and employment law as well. Because of this opportunity to be a part of such a transformational time at Walmart, I was able to quickly identify workplace issues and provide remedial and preventative measures for workplaces across the country.

Since that first day as an intern in Walmart's legal department, I've heard it all and seen it all with regard to every aspect of the workplace: managers, employees, HR, vendors, consultants, and customers. (Yes, workplaces are responsible for the conduct of their customers too!) But what stood out the most were my conversations about the ambiguity of workplace laws. Every law that seems to be black and white is simply anything but that. When you look at federal workplace statutes, they throw words out that have different meanings to every reader. Some common words we find ourselves coming across are: reasonable (that's probably the most frequent), necessary, legitimate, hostile, pretext, severe, serious, pervasive, adverse, offensive, neutral... did I say reasonable? What's reasonable to you may not be reasonable to me, or to a judge. As a manager or an organizational leader, you don't know if your actions are reasonable until one of your employees alleges that it is not. Then, you may have to pay tens of thousands of dollars for a judge or agency to tell you who's right and who's wrong!

This list of scenarios can be confusing and it may cause you to feel uncertain in your role as a leader or employee in the workplace. As a leader, you may often ask yourself, "Am I breaking any employment laws?" As an employee, you may often ask yourself, "Are my employee rights being violated?" My experiences witnessing the uncertainty and misinterpretation of workplace law inspired me to write this book *You Can't Do That at Work! 100 Common Legal Mistakes that Managers Make.*

I have experience working through the most complex workplace issues that have arisen in years, in some of America's largest organizations. I am called upon daily to share my expertise with both organizational leaders and employees on what is and is not lawful conduct at work. This book consists of accounts of my practical experience working in corporate legal and HR departments, working as a consult, and as an academic scholar in labor and employment law. Beyond the academic and corporate settings, I've had a 360-degree experience of the workplace, from being a leader without training to working for a leader without training. I have also been an employee whose workplace rights have been violated. Through the stories that I heard along the way, the court cases that have been decided, the opinion letters and guidance written by federal regulatory agencies, and my very own experiences, I have identified a list of the top 100 common legal mistakes that managers make that ultimately violate federal labor and employment discrimination laws.

This book by is by no means intended to give legal advice to its readers; its purpose is to go beyond the typical employment law handbook through storytelling, analysis, and a little humor. By the end of this book, you should gain an understanding that organizational policies do not shape organizational culture; the values, behaviors, and accepted conduct of management and leadership do. Creating an organizational culture that is inclusive and intolerant of discriminatory harassing and bullying is ultimately what mitigates legal liability. The goal of this book is for each reader, no matter their role in an organization, to be inspired to mitigate unlawful conduct in the workplace by having the confidence to say *You Can't Do That at Work!*

Navigating This Book

You Can't Do That at Work explores 100 common mistakes that managers make in regard to violating federal labor and employment laws; however, it does not discuss every potential federal workplace law that can be violated. The areas explored in this book are situations, challenges, and experiences that I have managed or helped organizations to manage that commonly cause confusion and challenges for employees and managers alike. It is also important to note that most states have laws that expand protections for employees well beyond federal statutes. But remember, states cannot write laws that give employees fewer protections than are provided by federal law. Finally, this book only addresses federal workplace laws that impact organizations in the private sector. At the beginning of each chapter of this book, I will outline the common mistakes that managers make as they relate to each topic. Then I will delve into a deeper analysis of how these mistakes put organizations at risk.

Part I - Harassment and Discrimination

Preventing harassment and discrimination is much more complicated than providing annual sexual harassment training to managers (which unfortunately is the only training on labor and employment that most managers get). This section explores primarily how harassment and discrimination can occur as a result of decisions and statements made by middle managers that most often have unintended consequences. This section will highlight common mistakes that managers make as it relates to: allowing managers to engage in intimidating and bullying conduct at work, workplace torts, age discrimination, sexual orientation and gender identity discrimination, religious accommodations, English-speaking-only workplace rules, ban the box, and reverse discrimination.

Part II - Health and Wellness at Work

Federal law provides employees with many protections if they are disabled, become disabled, or need time away from work for their own serious health conditions or those of their family members. While job-protected leaves and disability accommodations are beneficial for maintaining a healthy workforce and access to work for the disabled, because of the intersect of the Family and Medical Leave Act (FMLA) and the Americans with Disabilities Act (ADA), they can also be administratively burdensome and challenging to manage. This section will review common mistakes that managers make navigating the tangled web of the ADA, the FMLA, and the Pregnancy Discrimination Act (PDA), and provide guidance on how to effectively create wellness programs that are in compliance with the Genetic Information Nondiscrimination Act (GINA).

Part III - Wage and Hour

The year 2015 brought the Fair Labor Standards Act to the forefront of strategic priorities for organizations. As a new overtime rule was proposed on the federal level, organizations went into chaos auditing and revising job descriptions and reclassifying employees. Even before the proposed overtime rule was announced, the misclassification of employees continues to plague organizations. The ramifications of a misclassified employee can be unpaid compensable time and meal and rest break violations, which can lead to astronomical penalties. This section will analyze the common mistakes that managers make with misclassifying employees, compensable and non-compensable time, unpaid internships, independent contractors, joint employment, and pay equity in the workplace.

Part IV- Protected Concerted Activity

The usage of social media by employees has made it considerably easier for organizations to be liable for violations of workplace laws even when their employees are not on their premises or on the clock! The National Labor Relations Board continues to expand its interpretation of "protected concerted activity" to include an employee's ability to discuss the terms and conditions of employment on social media (even if it means disparaging their boss) and the right to be unhappy at work among other things. This section will examine the common mistakes that managers make as they relate to what is and what is not protected concerted activity and union organizing.

Part V - Unlawful Retaliation

Unlawful retaliation made up almost half of all claims filed with the Equal Employment Opportunity Commission (EEOC) in 2015. This is probably the case because an individual can have a successful claim even if their original complaint of discrimination was not legitimate. After an employee (or candidate or former employee) complains of harassment or discrimination, any unwelcomed action by the organization can be perceived as retaliation. This section will discuss common mistakes that managers make not only with recognizing potential retaliatory conduct, but also how to address concerns about an employee's performance after they have reported alleged unlawful conduct.

Part VI: The Future of You Can't Do That at Work

This section looks at what lies ahead for federal and state labor and employment law. Although there are rarely sweeping changes or additions to federal workplace law, the passage of workplace laws in one state can easily invoke the domino effect for other states. This section will explore the current trends and developments in state workplace law, the potential impact of the policies and agenda of the recently elected President of the United States, and address the influence that organizational culture can have on mitigating legal risk.

PART I

HARASSMENT AND DISCRIMINATION

Chapter 1

THE EQUAL OPPORTUNITY JERK

Common mistakes that managers make:

1. Thinking workplace bullying has no legal ramifications
2. Not investigating complaints about "high-value" employees
3. Not knowing the exceptions to the employment-at-will doctrine
4. Believing not everyone is in a protected class
5. Not auditing employee handbooks and practices for potential disparate impact
6. Using the Bona Fide Occupational Qualification (BFOQ) exception as a non-legitimate reason to discriminate against a protected class
7. Not training managers on the prevention of harassment and discrimination in the workplace
8. Not knowing that a person can be the recipient of unwelcomed, hostile conduct even if they are not the one being harassed
9. Not closing the loop with employees who have complained of harassment and discrimination

10. Believing that as long as the decision maker is in the same protected class as the complainer, there can be no discrimination
11. Using subjective criteria for hiring decisions
12. Not using panel interviews for hiring decisions
13. Using pretext as a defense to a discrimination claim
14. Not having a credible department
15. Transferring or suspending a complaining employee pending an investigation
16. Being unfamiliar with state tort laws that can be utilized as an alternative to filing a discrimination claim with the EEOC or State Civil Rights Agency
17. Failing to take action against or retain a negligent or dangerous supervisor, or failing to provide a safe workplace
18. Allowing harassing conduct that is so outrageous that it can be considered intentional infliction of emotional distress
19. Believing that employees leave managers, not organizations
20. Settling with those who sue rather than being proactive about preventing discrimination claims
21. Not tracking data that can provide insight about employee engagement

The Equal Opportunity Jerk at Work: You probably know one well. They lead by fear and intimation and more likely than not, they are a bully or a "corporate psychopath," as some refer to them. Typically, they are high performers. The

EEOC recently conducted a study on workplace harassment[1] and identified "workplace[s] with 'high-value' employees" as being particularly vulnerable to systemic harassment. These "high-value" employees achieve organizational goals and are considered the "rainmakers" for organizations. Because of their ability to meet and even exceed expectations, they can get away with almost anything because they have the ability to create an illusion of winning. If they are truly a "corporate psychopath," "their polish, charm, cool decisiveness, and fondness for the fast lane—are easily, and often, mistaken for leadership qualities."[2] When someone complains about their conduct, the answer typically is, "they treat everyone that way" or better yet, they have pulled the veil everyone's eyes so much that no one believes they could be harmful.

We've seen this all too often within college athletic departments. The "high-value" college coaches who have winning records, fill the stadium with screaming fans, and generate most of the school's revenue can get away with almost anything... even illegal things.

Colleges tend to turn their backs to complaints about them.

Why? There are two main reasons. The first is because no one wants to be the person who lets everyone down by disciplining or firing their winning coach. The second is that human resources departments sometimes feel they need to circumvent the hiring process or ignore complaints about

---

[1]   U.S. Equal Opportunity Employment Commission. 2016. "Select Taskforce on the Study of Harassment in the Workplace: Report of Co-Chairs Chai R. Feldblum & Victoria A. Lipnic." https://www.eeoc.gov/eeoc/task_force/harassment/report.cfm#_ftnref137.

[2]   Morse, G. 2004. "Executive Psychopaths." *Harvard Business Review* 80 (10). https://hbr.org/2004/10/executive-psychopaths.

them even though they are well aware that their decision could potentially lead to discrimination or harassment claims.

Both these scenarios played out at my alma mater, the University of Arkansas, and more famously at Penn State. The former scenario involved Coach Bobby Petrino, who was involved in a motorcycle crash one lovely spring afternoon in April 2012.

The crash resulted in minor injuries that under normal circumstances, would not have caused national concern. However, it was revealed Coach Petrino had an additional passenger on his bike, his mistress, Jessica Dorrell. Not only was Jessica his mistress, but she was also an employee in the athletic department hired by Coach Petrino.

During the hiring process, Coach Petrino circumvented the usual hiring process that required all jobs to be posted for 30 days. Although the University's Office of Equal Employment Opportunity warned that a deviation in the process could potentially make a recruiting error with the NCAA rules and regulations, the waiver was reluctantly granted.

It was later revealed that not only was Petrino engaged in a romantic, intimate relationship with Jessica, but that other, more qualified candidates were overlooked for the position. Ultimately, Petrino was fired, Jessica received a settlement, the HR department lost credibility, and the school was exposed and embarrassed.

High-value employees are not limited to those who rake in large amounts of money for organizations; high-value employees are also those who are near and dear to the leadership at an organization. Penn State and the now-deceased Coach Joe Paterno are still under fire because of a sexual abuse scandal that rocked the school and the athletic department's reputation. Assistant Coach Jerry Sandusky has been convicted of multiple counts of sexual abuse of children from his charity, The Second Mile.

Some of the abuse took place on Penn State's campus. It was witnessed and reported to university officials and Coach Paterno. Through an independent investigation, it was revealed that university officials had known about the abuse since 1998 and collectively decided not to report it. As such, Jerry Sandusky continued the abuse for another 14 years.[3] Although this particular case is not reflective of unfair treatment of an employee, it is demonstrative of the potential ramifications of preferential treatment and/or what happens when organizations have a "good ole boys'" club in place.

Although there were reported and investigated incidents of abuse before 1999, Sandusky was allowed to retire and received a one-time, lump-sum payment of $168,000 and unlimited access to Penn State's athletic facilities, where the abuse continued for years.

I have to ask this question: If the same transgression was reported about an employee whose name wasn't as well-known across the Penn State community, whose actions would not have had such an impact on the reputation of the athletic department, and who was not the close friend, if not best friend, of the famous Coach Paterno, would Penn State be in the mess it is in today?

More recently, stories have been circulating about the behind-the-scenes scandal at Wells Fargo Bank, where managers would bully employees to the point of illness to make sales goals. They would threaten their jobs and embarrass them in

---

[3]   CNN Library. 2017. "Penn State Scandal Fast Facts." *CNN* March 6, 2017. http://www.cnn.com/2013/10/28/us/penn-state-scandal-fast-facts/.

front of colleagues. Although the now-ousted CEO John Stumpf has denied that this culture was created at the top and has asserted he was unaware of the misdeeds of a "few" managers, it is reported that 5,300 employees were fired due to shady dealings. Furthermore, dozens of employees claimed that they were fired after reporting this illegal conduct. Although in this example the conduct by the managers at Wells Fargo was not just unethical, but illegal, that is not always the case. Every day there are managers, leaders, coaches, business owners, and other people of power who are engaging in disruptive, unethical, harassing conduct. Oftentimes, the conduct by the same group does not always appear at face value to be illegal, but rather just noncompliant with an organization's ethical and moral standards. However, by allowing this kind of conduct to exist, organizations not only can face legal consequences, but the conduct can also have a destructive impact on the health, engagement, and image an organization's greatest asset—its employees.

The origin of the Equal Opportunity Jerk stems from a principle that is recognized in the United States called the employment-at-will doctrine. The employment-at-will doctrine simply states that an employee or an employer can terminate the employment relationship at any time for good, bad, or no cause at all. While not recommended, I could, as a manager, walk into my office tomorrow and tell my assistant that her services are no longer needed; she would be free to leave, and I need offer no explanation. She, likewise, could do the same without consequence.

If your eyebrows are raised and the employment-at-will doctrine sounds a little too good to be true, you are right! There are actually four exceptions that practically deem the employment-at-will doctrine moot. We will discuss three of those exceptions briefly then elaborate on how the fourth one serves as the platform of how the concept of the Equal Opportunity Jerk earned its name.

Exception 1: Express Contract

If an employee and employer have entered into an employment contract that has a start and end date, specifies the obligations of both parties, and what breaches that agreement, then that employee is not at-will. Another example of an express contract in the workplace, and the most common one, is a collective bargaining agreement between an organization and a labor union. In the case of a collective bargaining agreement, the employees who are covered under the agreement are not at-will employees and can only be terminated for cause.

Exception 2: Implied Contract

An implied, or implicit, contract is one in which there has been an oral or implicit agreement of continued employment. A frequent example I like to give is the case where an employer makes a verbal job offer to a candidate in California with a start date of one month from the offer. The candidate in California reasonably relies on the employer's offer and quits her job and sells her house only to be told two days before she is to move to New York and start her new job that the position was cancelled due to budget cuts. The California job candidate can then argue that there was an implied contract that she reasonably relied on and suffered detrimentally as a result. The most common example of an implied contract is an employee handbook, which some employees have argued creates an implied contract as only violations of the handbook should result in an involuntary termination.

Exception 3: Public Policy

The public policy exception of the employment-at-will doctrine is probably the most difficult to understand – or explain! To make it as simple as possible, it would be a violation of public policy to terminate an employee because of their refusal to violate the law; for exercising a statutory obligation; for exercising a constitutional or statutory right; or, the most complicated one, for doing something the general public considers sycophantic or not worthy of discharge.

Here is an example: John works for Susan. John is a great employee with no record of performance or disciplinary issues. John's wife is a police officer. John's wife arrests Susan's husband for drinking and driving. Susan fires John because of the arrest. John could argue that it is against public policy for his police officer wife to be concerned with who she is arresting because her husband may be fired!

Exception 4: Discrimination and Harassment

The three above exceptions to the employment-at-will doctrine are not all recognized in every state, but every state and federal court agrees that employers are not at-will to discriminate against an employee due to their membership in a protected class.

Protected classes are determined by a number of federal (and state) laws. In this section, we will only cover federal employment anti-discrimination laws that are enforceable by the Equal Employment Opportunity Commission (EEOC)[4], the federal agency that regulates and enforces the laws that are outlined in the following chart.

FEDERAL LAW	PROTECTED CLASS COVERED	PROHIBITED CONDUCT
Title VII of the Civil Rights Act of 1964 (applies to employers with 15 or more employees)	Race, color, national origin, religion, sex	Discrimination is prohibited in any facet of employment, including hiring, firing, pay, job assignments, promotions, layoffs, training, fringe benefits, and any other term or condition of employment
Age Discrimination in Employment Act (applies to employers with 20 or more employees)	Age: applicants and employees 40 and over	Same as above
Pregnancy Discrimination Act (applies to employers with 15 or more employees)	Pregnancy, childbirth, or a medical condition related to pregnancy or childbirth. (Applicants and employees)	Same as above
Equal Pay Act (applies to employers covered under the FLSA)	Men and women	Requires that men and women in the same workplace be given equal pay for equal work

---

[4]   More information about the Equal Opportunity Employment Commission is available at www.eeoc.gov.

FEDERAL LAW	PROTECTED CLASS COVERED	PROHIBITED CONDUCT
Americans with Disabilities Act (ADA); Rehabilitation Act (applies to employers with 15 or more employees)	Applicants and employees with disabilities	Same as above
Genetic Information Nondiscrimination Act (GINA) (applies to employers with 15 or more employees)	Applicant, employee, applicant/employee genetic information	Same as above

Review the chart listing the federal anti-discrimination laws and which protected classes that they protect. Now, put a check mark next to the protected classes that you belong to. Everyone reading this book should have at least three marks.

You won't believe the number of times I have asked my employment law students to raise their hands if they are not in a protected class, and a young, white male raises his hand. It is a big misconception that anti-discrimination laws only cover minorities, women, and disabled people in the workplace. The fact of the matter is that everyone is a member of at least three protected classes: sex, race, and national origin.

There are four theories of unlawful discrimination and harassment in the workplace.

1. Disparate treatment - The *intentional* discrimination of a person because of their membership in a protected class.

This discrimination could be because of pure prejudice and/or bias or could be purposefully intentional. For instance, an organization may place a job posting for a female correction officer to guard female prisoners at a correctional facility. In this case, I am able to intentionally discriminate against male applicants due to safety considerations and the ability to perform searches of female inmates. However, in order to do this, I must prove that my intentional discrimination is due to Bona Fide Occupational Qualification (BFOQ). However, to make the determination that the need for a female-only correctional officer was a BFOQ, I would need to show that:

a)   the job qualification is reasonably necessary to the essence of its business; and

b)   that "sex is a legitimate proxy for determining" whether a candidate for the position has the necessary job qualifications.

In making this determination, the organization must determine that the decision was the outcome of reasonable decision making.

An example of when using sex as a BFOQ is not a reasonable decision would be if an organization posted a job for a female-only receptionist. Although the organization may believe that it is their customer's preference to hear a female voice when calling, customer preference is not a consideration when determining BFOQs.

BFO-HOOTERS!

My favorite BFOQ case is HOOTERS. You know, the restaurant where you can get delicious chicken wings that just so happen to be served by scantily clad women?

Ever wonder how they get away with their female-waitresses-only policy? Is being a woman really a BFOQ for waiting tables? I think not!

Hooters was able to suc-cessfully argue that their women-waitress-only policy was reasonably necessary to the normal operation of the particular business or exer-cise. They were able to compare themselves to companies that hire actors and models that are able to discriminate because they offer their customers enter-tainment and an experience, not just burgers and fries.

But, guys, no need to fret! You can still get a job at Hooters as a table busser or in the kitchen!

2.   Disparate impact - When an organization has a facially neutral policy that has an adverse impact against members of a protected class (unintentional discrimination). In order to prove disparate impact, the policy must adversely impact 4/5 of the protected class.

What does this mean? Let's revisit our example of a job posting for a female correctional officer. If it was the policy of the correctional facility to not just hire a female correctional officer for that job, but for all correctional officer positions within a female correctional facility, then that policy would have a disparate impact on the male applicants for that position. The correctional facility would need to prove that there was a legitimate business reason for their policy that all correctional officers at the female prison are female.

In this case, the prison would argue that female officers were exclusively necessary to prevent sexual assaults, for privacy for female inmates, and to be able to conduct searches of the female inmates. However, male applicants would argue that the exclusivity is not a legitimate business decision as there are other roles and responsibilities within the prison that male correction officers could do that would not involve those duties stated by the prison.

For instance, male officers could supervise gym activities, visitation, and religious activities to name a few. Therefore, in this case, a policy of hiring only female correctional officers would probably fail.[5] It is important to add that for a claim of disparate impact to be successful, the plaintiff must provide statistical evidence of discrimination.

3.   Hostile work environment - Unwelcome conduct based on a person's protected class that is so severe and pervasive that a reasonable person would consider hostile, intimidating, and/or abusive.

---

5   Teamsters Local Union No. 117 v. Washington Department of Corrections (2008).

Some examples of conduct that can rise to the level of being hostile are according to the EEOC: offensive jokes, slurs, epithets or name calling, physical assaults or threats, intimidation, ridicule or mockery, insults or put-downs, offensive objects or pictures, and interference with work performance.

A hostile work environment can be created not just by those in a supervisory position, but also by co-workers, customers, and vendors. A person can be the recipient of unwelcome, hostile conduct even if they are not the one being harassed. There does not need to be a tangible employment action connected to a hostile work environment claim.

Although a hostile work environment can be created for someone due to their membership in any protected class, it is most often reported in sexual harassment cases.

4. Quid pro quo - This for that. A supervisor offers to give an employee or job applicant something favorable (a job, a raise, a promotion, etc.) in exchange for a sexual favor. Quid pro quo harassment can also occur when a manager threatens to not hire, fire, or not promote, etc. if the employee or applicant does not yield to their sexual advances.

Proving Harassment and Discrimination

For an employee or job applicant to prove a claim of discrimination and/or harassment, they must first prove that the discrimination and/or harassment was based upon his or her protected class as described in the federal anti-discrimination laws chart.

In my many years of conducting countless investigations into situations in which an employee has accused his or her manager of unlawful harassment and discrimination, I am usually able to bucket my findings to one of the following outcomes:

1. There was no unlawful harassment or discrimination
2. There was unlawful harassment or discrimination
3. There was harassment, but it was lawful

There was no unlawful harassment or discrimination. Some employees will come to HR and use the term harassment and discrimination when they do not agree with a disciplinary action, or didn't get a desired job or transfer, are simply being held accountable for job performance. I am able to determine that there was no unlawful harassment and/or discrimination only after the manager is able to articulate a legitimate, non-discriminatory reason for the action that the employee is alleging was discriminatory. These reasons could include that there was a more qualified candidate, that the complaining employee had documented sub-par performance, or that the complaining employee simply did not meet the minimum qualifications for the position just to name a few.

There was unlawful harassment and discrimination. Unfortunately, during my career, many investigations have led to the conclusion that some managers have in fact have intentionally discriminated against employees because of their membership in a protected class. I cannot outline every scenario in this book, but when I am investigating a claim of discrimination, I use the framework as outlined in *McDonnell Douglas v. Green.*[6] This is also the framework that is used to determine if unlawful discrimination has occurred when the claim is filed at the EEOC and/or federal court.

Let's take for an example an employee who walks into HR claiming that they did not receive a promotion because of their protected class (most employees will not use the term "protected class," they will just state it). Here is what the *McDonnell Douglas* framework would look like in this instance. Essentially, it is a three-part test:

1. First, determine if the employee has a prima facie case for discrimination. To establish a prima facie case:
   - The employee is in a protected class (check!)
   - The employee was qualified (and in this case, eligible under the company's policies) for the promotion
   - The employee did not get the promotion
   - An employee outside of the employee's protected class got the promotion. Here, if the employee is saying he was discriminated against because he is male and a female got the job, assuming the other elements of the prima facie case were established, we move on step 2.

---

6   McDonell Douglas Corp. v. Green, 411 U.S. 792 (1973).

2.   Now the manager must articulate a legitimate, non-discriminatory reason for why the employee did not get the job. Some examples of legitimate, non-discriminatory reasons could be:
   -   Although the employee was qualified, I promoted a more qualified employee (of course the manager would need to specifically articulate the differences in qualifications).
   -   The employee didn't interview well. (Panel interviews and/or having employees and applicants interview with more than one person helps to eliminate bias and discrimination when hiring and/or promoting employees).
3.   Once the manager has articulated his or her legitimate business reason for not hiring the employee, the employee now has the opportunity to call their bluff. Or in other words, say that the manager's reason for not promoting them was pretext for discrimination. For example, the employee could bring to your attention to the fact that the last five promotions by this manager were females.

If that is the case, then I would dig deeper into the manager's hiring and promotion history and determine that this manager has never promoted a male, although they could have hired many qualified males.

Using the McDonnell Douglas three-part test as part of your investigation framework will help you to conduct a thorough, consistent investigation which will help you to reach the right conclusions internally while possibly mitigating the employee

YOU **CAN'T** DO THAT **AT WORK**

from going to seek help from outside counsel to resolve their workplace concerns.

There was harassment, but it was lawful. Meaning yes, the employee was in fact being harassed or discriminated against, but it was not necessarily based on his protected class. This is where we find our Equal Opportunity Jerk at Work.

The Equal Opportunity Jerk at Work believes that as long his harassing, intimidating, and hostile behavior is aimed at all employees regardless of their protected class, he is then protected from unlawful harassment and discrimination claims. Unfortunately, he is not alone in his thoughts. Excuses are made for him and when someone complains about his behavior, the response is, "Don't take it personally, he treats everyone that way." Many organizations believe that they have no recourse for addressing his behavior. He produces results, reaches organizational goals, and hasn't broken any laws or maybe not any workplace policies. But nothing could be further from the truth.

Let's take the case of a secretary at a manufacturing company who was subjected to harassment from her recently divorced boss. At first, the secretary's boss began to sexually harass her by making unwanted sexual comments and standing too close to her, among other things. However, when she refused his advances, he began to make physical abuse threats including the insinuation of choking and killing her. He even went so far as to say he wanted to see her in a coffin! When she complained to Human Resources, they responded by transferring her to another job in which she was given no work and was eventually terminated from the company. She sued for sexual harassment and retaliation.

The company used the Equal Opportunity Jerk defense, citing that her boss had threatened to choke and kill male employees as well. (Why is his company ok with this?) The lower court bought the Equal Opportunity defense and dismissed her claims. However, on appeal, the appeal court cited another case that stated that sex-based discrimination cannot be "short-circuited by the mere fact that both men and women are involved." Although the manager harassed the male workers on occasion, that was not enough of a defense that the female workers were not the primary targets.[7] The Equal Opportunity Jerk defense had failed! YOU CAN'T DO THAT AT WORK!

Although in the previous case, the employee was able to defeat the Equal Opportunity Jerk under a Title VII[8] cause of action, victims of Equal Opportunity Jerks have little-known legal options in addition to the employment discrimination statutes found in our chart.

Workplace Torts

Many employees and employers are unaware that an employee who is suffering under the guise of "lawful" harassment at work may still have legal recourses other than federal anti-discrimination statutes. There are little-known or forgotten avenues that an employee may pursue in their respective state courts other than filing a federal equal employment opportunity claim. These avenues are called workplace torts. A tort is an

---

7   Kaytor v. Electric Boat Corp., No. 09-1859 (2d Cir. 2010).

8   Information about Title VII of the Civil Rights Act of 1964 is available at www.eeoc.gov/laws/statutes/titlevii.cfm.

infringement or wrongful act committed in the workplace that can also result in civil legal liability for both the manager or supervisor and the organization. Common workplace torts are:

Fraud: If a manager or organization misrepresented information or facts to you that you or someone else reasonably relied on to your detriment, that could be considered fraud. An example of fraud in the workplace could be that a manager tells an employee that he should find another job because the company will be closing soon when in fact there is no intent for the company to close. If the employee relies on that information and finds another job and quits, he could sue his employer for fraud.

Defamation: An organization can "defame" an employee if it communicates a lie or makes a false accusation about the employee, either orally or in writing, to a third person, which causes damage to the employee's reputation. Workplace defamation claims are most often made when an employer maliciously provides false information to a potential employer about a former or current employee during a reference check.

As it relates to providing references, simple mistakes of miscommunication are not defamation as the person providing the reference must have acted with malice and intent to deceive. Additionally, the employee must prove that their reputation was actually damaged by the statements. To avoid defamation claims, many organizations now only give limited information about an employee's employment history, which usually only includes start and end date of employment, job title, and salary history. Some organizations also include whether or not the employee is re-hirable, however even then many don't cross that line.

False Imprisonment: False imprisonment occurs when an employee's freedom of movement is impeded without that employee's permission and without legal justification. An example of this would be if a manager calls an employee into their office and refuses to allow them to leave (by locking the door or threats). Some things to consider when determining whether or not someone has been falsely imprisoned is the length of time the employee is held against their will, the reason for the detention, and the manner in which their freedom to leave is impeded.

Negligence: The Equal Opportunity Jerk can put organizations at risk for claims of negligent hiring, negligent supervision or retention of a dangerous employee, or failure to provide a safe workplace if it has knowledge of tortious conduct of the manager and fails to take action. Although the supervisor's behavior may not seem to be unlawful because "they're treating everyone that way," this harassing behavior can still be unlawful! The most applicable to our Equal Opportunity Jerk, however, is the negligent intentional infliction of emotional distress, also known as the tort of outrage.

A claim of negligent intentional infliction of emotional distress is very difficult to prove, but if an employee chooses to file such a claim, they must prove the following:

1. that the conduct was extreme and outrageous conduct,
2. the conduct intended to cause, or disregarded a substantial probability of causing, severe emotional distress,

3. there was a causal connection between the conduct and injury; and
4. caused severe emotional distress.

Conduct that is extreme and outrageous is difficult to prove, as past court cases have consistently demonstrated that criticism of an employee's job performance, aggressive interrogations, unwarranted reprimands, opposition to unemployment benefits, and/or excessive micromanaging alone is not considered outrageous conduct.

However, that is not to say an employee can never prevail in an intentional infliction of emotional distress claim. One instance was when a clerk in a Texas office at the Ford Motor Credit Company asked for a transfer to the collection department. She was told that "women usually don't go into that department" and a less-qualified male was hired. After she complained about the alleged discrimination, management began to retaliate by frequently changing her desk in the administrative department, assigned her more work than the other clerks, and subjected her to further unfair harassment. The nail in the coffin was when her supervisor, who had access to company checks, placed some of them in her purse to make it look like she had stolen them. The Texas court considered the conduct by her employer "outrageous" and said YOU CAN'T DO THAT AT WORK. Specifically, the court noted that the conduct of targeting her criminal liability was unlawful and outrageous. The court did note, however, that without the "checks" incident that the conduct by the employee would not have been "outrageous" and would have been in the scope of employment, although it could be considered unfair and discriminatory.

The Equal Employment Opportunity Commission (EEOC) and the courts define **"sexual harassment"** as unwelcome behavior of a sexual nature that:

- Explicitly or implicitly affects a term or condition of an individual's employment
- Unreasonably interferes with an employee's work performance
- Creates an intimidating, hostile, or offensive work environment

Sexual harassment can be:

- Physical, including unwelcome touching or gesturing
- Verbal, including unwelcome requests for a date or sexual favors or lewd remarks or sounds
- Visual, including unwelcome exposure to sexual photos, cartoons, or drawings

The conduct must be unwelcomed and severe and pervasive.

Cases that involve unlawful sexual harassment are the most common successful intentional infliction of emotional distress cases.

Actionable sexual harassment cases in the workplace fall into two categories as previously discussed: quid pro quo and hostile work environment. Organizations are strictly liable in quid pro quo claims when an organization has delegated authority to managers to make decisions affecting an employee's terms and conditions of employment. However, in hostile work environment claims, employers are not held strictly liable for their supervisors' and/or managers' actions. Instead, courts look to whether or not the employer has taken reasonable steps to prevent the harassment, whether or not the employer took prompt action to remedy any reported harassment, and what steps it took to remedy the matter.

If organizations fail or make an unsatisfactory attempt at the preceding, they may not only be liable for the conduct under Title VII, but also find themselves defending an intentional infliction of emotional distress claim.

This was the case when an office manager at Smith Produce, owned by Syndex Corporation, was the unwelcome recipient of sexual advances by her supervisor. While they at first had a cordial, professional relationship, the relationship began to change when her supervisor began to discuss sexual problems he was having with his wife, tried to kiss her, touch her several times, rubbed her neck, poked her, and then changed his attitude toward her when she refused his request for sex. The court held that YOU CAN'T DO THAT AT WORK because the conduct involved was obscene, physically assaultive, and vulgar, or better yet – outrageous![9]

In the previous cases, the employers have been found to be liable for intentional infliction of emotional distress while also violating Title VII laws. There have also been times when employees have successfully won intentional infliction of emotional distress absent a Title VII claim. In a particularly interesting case, an employee was able to successfully argue intentional infliction of emotional distress when her employer exposed her to secondhand cigarette smoke for fifteen years, causing her severe breathing problems. Although she provided

---

9   Bushell v. Dean 781 S.W.2d 652 (1989).

evidence to her employer of the harm to her health, her employer still refused to establish a tobacco-free workplace policy![10]

Practical Considerations

When employees are bullied or harassed at work, they often feel as if they have limited options. The first, and probably the ideal option, would be to file a complaint with human resources. Human resources should thoroughly investigate the claims and determine appropriate action. However, as discussed earlier in this chapter, there could be many reasons why appropriate action may not be taken.

The employee may then elect to take the second option: find another job and resign. There is an old saying out there that employees don't leave their companies, they leave their manager. I don't agree with this saying.

If an organization keeps a bad manager around, especially knowing that this manager is toxic and a bully, the employee is leaving that organization because they don't have the courage, the knowledge, and/or just don't care about "the little guys."

The third option is for the employee to stick around and stick it out. However, in this case, the employee is likely to become disengaged. At this point, they have probably lost their drive, ambition, and hope. Negativity begins to build and will likely spread to others, which will create more toxicity, negativity, and unproductivity. Additionally, as we all know, there are other implications of a disengaged employee: low productivity, absenteeism, less regard for safety, and much more.

---

10   Carroll v. Tennessee Valley Authority, 697 F. Supp. 508 (D.D.C. 1988).

The last option is that the employee can file a discrimination and/or harassment charge with the EEOC (or state agency that enforces equal employment opportunity in the workforce). When an employee is terminated without what they perceive to be an adequate explanation or investigation, or if they believe that they are being treated unfairly at work (either lawful or unlawful), and have had no success with support or compassion from their leadership team or human resources, they will often feel as if they have no other choice to but file a claim of discrimination.

Oftentimes, an employee knows their chances of prevailing in court are unlikely, but because of the mental and possibly physical anguish they have endured under the Equal Opportunity Jerk at work, they will take that chance with hopes that the organization will settle with them to avoid the time and cost of going through litigation. And they may be right!

According to a report released by the EEOC, there were 89,385 charges of workplace discrimination that the agency received in fiscal year 2015. However, of those 89,385, the EEOC only filed 142 merit lawsuits. However, the EEOC was able to successfully resolve 7,846 disputes through its mediation program in 2014.

Organizations know that litigation can be costly, time-consuming, and stressful on the work environment. So when they receive the charge of discrimination from the EEOC, they will often be more than willing to settle through mediation to avoid unwanted cost and time, risk unveiling other unknown unlawful and/or embarrassing behavior, and draw unwanted negative media attention that these suits can bring with them.

So what can organizations do to address Equal Opportunity Jerks at Work?

- Investigate all claims of harassment and discrimination that are brought to your attention, even if you believe that the claims of harassment or discrimination will not yield corroborative evidence.
- Track not only complaints about harassment and discrimination, but also track other metrics that indicate employee disengagement. Some of these additional metrics can include: high turnover, excess absenteeism, workers' compensation claims, and low productivity.
- Ensure that your human resources department has developed a reputation of credibility and trust within your organization. Employees are likely to skip your formal internal complaint process and file a charge with a state civil rights agency or the EEOC if they think that their complaints will be ignored, not taken seriously, or if HR always sides with management.

It can be extremely challenging to convince an organization not to tolerate the behavior of their Equal Opportunity Jerk. But the impact of an Equal Opportunity Jerk at Work can be detrimental to an organization, costing it upward of 550 million workdays a year according to the American Psychological Association. Additionally, only 32% of employees working in the U.S. are engaged at work with five out of the top ten drivers of disengagement being attributed to bad management. Despite the indisputable quantitative and qualitative data that demonstrates the influence that bad leadership can have on an organization, these stories play out time and time again, and the Equal Opportunity Jerk continues to prevail. Keeping bad managers around can also have hidden costs and dangers by way of high turnover, absenteeism, and high healthcare expenses. When employees are stressed, that can lead to medical problems that can put organizations on the hook for even more legal liabilities, which we will discuss later in the book, such as FMLA, ADA, and workers' compensation claims. Armed with this knowledge, if you're an organizational leader, will you let the Equal Opportunity Jerk expose your organization to legal liability? Let them run off your top-performing employees? Damage the positive reputation that you've worked so hard to establish? Or, better yet, knowing that your employees are reading this book and now know that they have avenues to fight against the Equal Opportunity Jerk, are you going to let them? Or are you going to tell that Equal Opportunity Jerk: YOU CAN'T DO THAT AT WORK!

The charge numbers (FY 2015) show the following breakdowns by basis alleged:

- Retaliation: 39,757 (44.5% of all charges filed)
- Race: 31,027 (34.7%)
- Disability: 26,968 (30.2%)
- Sex: 26,396 (29.5%)
- Age: 20,144 (22.5%)
- National Origin: 9,438 (10.6%)
- Religion: 3,502 (3.9%)
- Color: 2,833 (3.2%)
- Equal Pay Act: 973 (1.1%)
- Genetic Information Non-Discrimination Act: 257 (0.3%)
- These percentages add up to more than 100 because some charges allege multiple bases.

Chapter 2

DISPARATE IMPACT REVISITED

Common mistakes that managers make:

22. Not conducting criminal background checks as they misunderstand "ban-the-box" legislation
23. Discriminating against potential job candidates due to the fact they have a criminal record
24. Having policies that have a disparate impact against those with criminal convictions
25. Not complying with the Fair Credit Reporting Act (FCRA) by not allowing those with criminal records time to respond or dispute their record
26. Having blanket policies that prohibit hiring applicants with criminal records that are not job related
27. Only allowing workers to speak English in the workplace, refusing them the opportunity to speak their native language even when on break or during non-work time
28. Creating English-speaking only policies without business justification

Most organizations and managers do not intentionally violate employment discrimination laws, but rather have policies and practices in place that have unintended, yet unlawful consequences. As explained in the previous chapter, organizations may have policies that on their face seem neutral, but may inadvertently create an adverse impact on a protected class. Again, disparate impact is unintentional discrimination, but unlike disparate treatment or intentional discrimination, it may take years to determine that the seemingly neutral criterion is realized. The general guideline to follow to determine whether or not an employment policy or practice has an adverse impact against a protected class is to determine whether it impacts 4/5 of the protected class. Let's explore how some seemingly neutral organizational policies and practices may unintentionally adversely impact a protected class.

Ban the Box? Criminal Arrest and Convictions

Approximately 65 million people in the United States have criminal records. Criminal records can include not only criminal convictions, but also arrests that do not result a conviction. 50% of black males are arrested by the age of 23. If they are looking to get a new job, about 92% of organizations will find out about their criminal records by conducting a criminal background check as a part of the hiring process. For some organizations, once they've learned about a job applicant's arrest or conviction, the job applicant is automatically rejected from being hired. Many states have taken notice of the effect of such practices and have taken action.

If you haven't heard the term "ban the box" yet, you are sure to soon. Ban-the-box laws prohibit employers from asking about an applicant's criminal arrests and convictions during the application process. While there isn't any current federal ban-the-box legislation, almost half of the states in the U.S. have "ban-the-box" or similar policies prohibiting public sector employers from asking about criminal convictions and arrests. About nine states also prohibit private employers from the same.

As of Dec 1, 2016, there are over 150 cities and counties and 24 states that have adopted "ban-the-box" type laws. Additionally, President Obama has also endorsed banning the box for federal agencies.

States with ban the box for public employers are:

CA, CO, CT, DE, GA, HI, IL, LA, MD, MA, MN, MO, NE, NJ, NM, NY, OH, OK, OR, RI, TN, VT, WI

States with ban the box for private employers are:

CT, HI, Il, MA, MN, NJ, OR, RI, VT

Proponents of "ban-the box" initiatives argue that those with a criminal record, especially ones that are from years ago and not job-related, deserve a second chance to work. If applicants with criminal convictions are given the opportunity to work, this will mitigate them from re-entering a life of crime and thereby finding themselves back in prison. By the time an employer identifies a candidate who is qualified for the job, interviews well, and extends a job offer, they have invested a lot of time and energy in that candidate. If during a post-job-offer background check it is revealed that the job candidate has a criminal conviction, the employer may think twice before revoking the offer. Why? Because at this point, the employer has gotten to know the candidate well, invested time in them, and has also invested significant monetary resources.

However, studies have shown that if an employer learns of a candidate's criminal conviction because they have checked the box next to "Have you ever been convicted of crime?" they may not even be given consideration. Some national private employers such as Walmart and Target agree with these sentiments and have banned the box absent explicit federal legislation.

In addition to state and local laws that have passed advocating for such policies, the EEOC is also a proponent of limiting the use of a job candidate's criminal record when making hiring decisions, citing that the use of such information could significantly disadvantage those in certain protected classes.[11] As discussed earlier, this could create a disparate impact.

Opponents of "ban-the-box" legislation disagree with the measures for almost the same reasons that it appeals to others, citing that a company has invested too much time, resources, and money in a candidate only to find out that the candidate has a criminal conviction *after* the job offer has been made.

Additionally, employers worry about the potential legal risk of hiring someone with a criminal record, especially if the person ends up causing harm to their employees, customers, patients, etc. As we all know, one of the main reasons that employers started to ask this question in the first place was because they have a common-law duty (see section on workplace torts) to avoid foreseeable risk to their employees, customers,

---

11   Further information about the EEOC's recommendations can be found at https://www.eeoc.gov/laws/guidance/arrest_conviction.cfm#IIIA.

vendors, patients, etc. To relieve some of the anxiety for being liable in tort for hiring someone with a criminal record, twelve states have laws that protect employers from such claims.

A common misconception is that ban-the-box legislation doesn't allow employers to run criminal background checks at all. However, this is not the case. Rather, ban-the-box laws require the criminal background check to be done later in the hiring process.

I know what you're going to ask next: "But what if something does show up in the criminal background check when it is completed?" Good question! The following is some guidance and consideration that will help employers to avoid both the legal implications of not asking about a candidate's arrest or criminal conviction during the hiring process at all, asking about a job candidate's arrest or criminal conviction either before or after a job offer has been extended, and what to do if it is determined that a job applicant does in fact have a criminal record.

Not Conducting a Background Check During the Hiring Process

According to a survey conducted by the Society of Human Resources Management (SHRM) in 2010, 7% of the employers that were surveyed reported that they do not conduct criminal background checks on any of their job applicants.[12] Assuming that these employers are not included in industries that have occupations where criminal background checks are required to be licensed professionals, these employers simply rely on

---

12   Society for Human Resources Management. 2010. "Conducting Criminal Background Checks" slide 3. http://www.slideshare.net/shrm/background-check-criminal?from=share_email.

their instincts, perhaps rely on personal referrals or references, or just take a risk.

However, as stated earlier, there are indeed some risks. These organizations expose themselves to increased theft, embezzlement, and fraud. Again, these employers are also exposed to claims of negligent hiring as they have a reasonable obligation to avoid foreseeable risk to other employees, customers, patients, vendors, etc. in the workplace. One of the primary ways that an employer can foresee harm is by conducting a criminal background check to catch a glimpse into a job applicant's previous conduct, both in and outside of the workplace. A comprehensive background check that revealed no prior criminal activity is a sure-fire defense to negligent hiring claims.

If a Job Application Asks a Candidate If They Have Been Arrested or Convicted of a Crime

You can avoid disparate treatment claims by ensuring that all applicants are treated equally when it is discovered that they have a criminal record. Uniform guidelines should include predetermined criteria for rejecting an application. Ensure that those in one protected class are not being rejected when those in another protected class who are similarly situated are not. In other words, if you decide not to hire a male applicant due to a conviction of domestic assault, you must make that same decision for a female with the same conviction.

You can also avoid disparate impact claims by ensuring that members of one protected class are not being adversely impacted by criminal conviction policies. Employers should frequently conduct a statistical analysis of their criminal background data to determine if a disparate impact against a protected class is present.

When the Job Applicant Has a Criminal Conviction or Arrest

The Fair Credit Reporting Act (FCRA), a federal law that also dictates the use of criminal background checks in the workplace, requires employers to provide job applicants with a pre-adverse action letter if they determine that it will take adverse action because of information found in a criminal background check. Employers must then give the applicant a reasonable timeframe to respond or dispute the findings of the criminal background check before a final decision not to hire.

For an employer to determine not to hire someone based upon their criminal record, they must prove that their policy is "job related and consistent with business necessity." The EEOC has provided specific guidance on determining whether or not an employer has shown that its policy "operates to effectively link specific criminal conduct, and its dangers, with the risks inherent in the duties of a particular position." Additionally, it identifies two circumstances in which employers can make this link:

- The employer validates the criminal conduct screen for the position in question per the Uniform Guidelines on Employee Selection Procedures[13] (Uniform Guidelines) standards (if data about criminal conduct as related to

---

13   29 CFR Part 1607 - Uniform Guidelines on Employee Selection Procedures (1978).

subsequent work performance is available and such validation is possible) and

- The employer develops a targeted screen considering at least the nature of the crime, the time elapsed, and the nature of the job (the three "Green" factors), and then provides an opportunity for an individualized assessment for people excluded by the screen to determine whether the policy as applied is job related and consistent with business necessity.

The Green Factors

In *Green v. Missouri Pacific Railroad*,[14] the employer had a policy of excluding any job candidates with a conviction of any crime other than a minor traffic offense. The case outlined three factors to determine whether or not this type of exclusion was job related and consistent with business necessity.

- The nature and gravity of the offense or conduct. Of course if someone is convicted of bank robbery, they probably won't ever be hired as a bank teller! Those convicted of child molestation won't get a job at a day care center, and so on.
- The time that has passed since the offense or conduct and/or completion of the sentence. If a job candidate was convicted of a crime 7 years ago and has had a clean record since, an employer should still consider them to for the

---

14   Green v. Missouri Pacific Railroad, 523 F.2d 1290 (8th Cir. 1975).

open position, even if the crime was job related. (Additionally, studies have proven that the likelihood that an employee would reoffend decreases with age!)

- The nature of the job held or sought - The EEOC offers four important factors to consider:
  - The nature of the job duties
  - Identification of the job's essential functions
  - The circumstances under which the job is performed
  - The environment in which the job duties are performed.

Practical Tips

1. Know your state and local laws on permissible criminal background checks. Some states and municipalities have "ban-the-box" types of legislation. Some say that you cannot ask about arrests at all, some specify the timeframe that you can look back at a criminal record, and some have additional "tests" that you must consider to determine job-relatedness and much more. Know your stuff!

2. While I do not go into detail about it in this book, you should also be familiar and compliant with the Fair Credit Reporting Act (FCRA) that also legislates not only the use of criminal background checks but driving records, credit checks, or any consumer report relied upon to make hiring decisions.

3.   Note that Title VII does not preempt federal statutes and other regulations that govern eligibility for occupational licenses and registrations such as those working in the healthcare, transportation, and financial industries.

4.   Eliminate blanket policies that exclude all candidates who have ever been arrested or convicted of a crime, even if there is no state or local law prohibiting you from doing so. These decisions should be analyzed on a case-by-case basis.

5.   Keep good records! The determination to make an adverse employment decision should be documented in detail and kept confidential. Remember to conduct frequent audits of adverse hiring decisions based upon criminal records to ensure that your organization is not running the risk of disparate treatment or disparate impact claims.

English-Only Workplaces

As the United States increases in diversity in the workplace, so have the number of discrimination claims based upon an employee's national origin. So much so, that the EEOC published new guidelines for employers to prevent national origin discrimination claims. The guidelines give similar guidance to those which have been previously discussed in this book regarding unlawful discrimination and harassment based upon a person's protected class. It also elaborates on a common question of whether or not a policy that prohibits employees from speaking any language other than English could create an adverse impact on the hiring of employees from multiple national origins.

Before embarking on answering that question, it is important to highlight the difference between race, color, and national origin discrimination as many employers (and employees) don't quite understand the difference between the three. Neither Title VII nor the EEOC defines the word "race" as it applies to the workplace, but the EEOC does refer to the definition provided by the Office of Budget Management (OBM) that identifies five categories of race:

- American Indian or Alaska Native;
- Asian; Black or African American;
- Native Hawaiian or other Pacific Islander;
- White;
- and one ethnicity category, Hispanic or Latino

"Color" is also not defined by Title VII or the EEOC, but the common meaning is understood to be

- pigmentation;
- complexion;
- skin shade;
- or tone

Although there is clearly an intersection between race and color, they are synonymous. In addition to race and color, discrimination is also prohibited when an employer bases an employment decision on an individual's place of origin, or ancestor's place of origin, because an individual has the physical, cultural, or linguistic characteristics of a national origin group. Because some people of the same national origin are often the same race (as in the case of Asian Americans), race and national origin frequently overlap. There are many intersectional discrimination scenarios that spin out of this that I won't go into detail about in this book, but an applicant or employee can easily bring a claim for race, color, and national origin discrimination based on the same facts. (Oh, and let's not forget to include religious discrimination in there!)

Many organizations, especially those that require a great deal of both oral and written communication, have English-only workplace rules. These rules can prove to be problematic as they can have the potential to violate Title VII, which was the case when the EEOC was awarded $700,000 on behalf of 13 Hispanic workers who were hired to speak Spanish to Spanish-speaking customers! Their employer, a former long-distance telephone operator service had an English-speaking-only policy that banned speaking any language other than English, even during non-working times such as lunch breaks, unless speaking to a non-English speaking customer. Many of the employees refused to sign the policy and some challenged the policy and were fired. YOU CAN'T DO THAT AT WORK!

In this case, the court emphasized the fact that English-speaking-only policies must be based on justified business needs. The court also rejected the employer's argument that the policy was needed to "improve communication" amongst workers, but rather the court stated that the policy did "quite the opposite... the policy served to create a disruption in the workplace and feelings of alienation and inadequacy by... proven performers."[15]

It is also appropriate to add to this section that federal law also prohibits discrimination based on an individual's citizenship or immigration status. The Immigration Reform and Control Act (IRCA) prohibits organizations hiring only U.S. citizens or lawful permanent residents. If an employee presents acceptable documentation that establishes their lawful eligibility to work in the U.S., an employer must accept such documentation and may not require additional documentation beyond what is required by law. Employees can choose which documentation they will present when completing an I-9 form. IRCA is regulated by the Department of Justice's Office of Special Counsel for Immigration-Related Unfair Employment Practices (OSC), Civil Rights Division.

Practical Considerations

Policies that limit an employee's ability to speak their native language should be reviewed to ensure that there is a legitimate business justification for such policies. Blanket policies that prohibit employees from speaking their language at all times can be viewed as discrimination based upon an employee's national origin. Policies that limit an employee's ability to speak their native language even during rest breaks during non-work times, such as meal breaks, should be eliminated.

---

15   U.S. Equal Employment Opportunity Commission. 2000. "Court Speaks: English Only Rule Unlawful; Awards EEEOC $700,000 For Hispanic Workers." https://www.eeoc.gov/eeoc/newsroom/release/9-19-00.cfm.

Avoiding Disparate Impact Claims

Most disparate impact claims are related to an employer's selection, hiring, and promotion processes and policies. As such, the Uniform Guidelines on Employee Selection Procedures (UGESP) were adopted jointly by the EEOC, the U.S. Department of Labor, and the U.S. Department of Justice to help employers avoid disparate impact claims. In these guidelines, a four-step process is outlined to help employers determine if their current practices could potentially result in a disparate impact claim:

1. Calculate the rate of selection for each group (divide the number of persons selected from a group by the number of applicants from that group).
2. Observe which group has the highest selection rate.
3. Calculate the impact ratios by comparing the selection rate for each group with that of the highest group (divide the selection rate for a group by the selection rate for the highest group).
4. Observe whether the selection rate for any group is substantially less (i.e., usually less than 4/5ths or 80%) than the selection rate for the highest group. If it is, adverse impact is indicated in most circumstances.

Additionally, the Supreme Court offered guidance when the City of New Haven attempted to design a test to be used for promotion considerations that was fair and would ensure that minority firefighters would have the opportunity for promotion. Despite including African Americans and Hispanic Americans on each "test" panel when designing the test, with the exception of two Hispanic candidates, the highest scoring candidates were all Caucasians.

As a result, the city decided not to use the test, fearing that they would face disparate impact claims from the African-American candidates. However, just the opposite happened. They were actually sued by the Caucasian and two Hispanic candidates for disparate treatment (intentional discrimination) because they were rejected due to their race.[16] The Supreme Court held that YOU CAN'T DO THAT AT WORK! They agreed with the plaintiffs when they argued that you cannot commit intentional discrimination in order to circumvent unintentional discrimination. Because the test was "job-related" or that "other, equally valid and less discriminatory tests were available," the results should have stuck!

Practical Considerations

- Employers should hire, promote, and establish policies without regard to a person's protected class.
- All selection tests, hiring and promotion processes, and other policies (such as English speaking only) should be validated to ensure that there is no potential for disparate impact liability.
- If it is determined that a selection process or policy does adversely impact a protected class, employers should determine whether there is an alternative selection method with less impact.
- Train managers on your selection practices and processes to ensure your organization is consistent.

---

16   Ricci v. DeStefano, 557 U.S. 557 (2009).

Chapter 3

SEXUAL ORIENTATION & GENDER-BASED DISCRIMINATION

Common mistakes that managers make:

29. Not understanding LGBT rights under federal law
30. Not respecting transgender employees
31. Discriminating against transgender employees by designating restrooms for them to use
32. Not creating a detailed plan for transitioning employees in the workplace
33. Not taking the steps to understand gender identity and appropriate terminology relating to it
34. Taking advantage of employees who have parental responsibilities in an unlawful way

Recently, more and more celebrities, professional athletes, and politicians have come out publicly revealing their sexual orientation and/or revealing that they identify with a gender that is different from their biological gender.

Bruce Jenner, the renowned Olympic champion and reality TV star, famously revealed that he was transitioning genders and officially changing his name to Caitlyn Jenner. She was praised for her braveness and as Caitlyn, has become an idol and champion for the transgender community. What's more, her employer, the E! Network, even went on to create her own reality show that would document her transition as she dealt with the challenges and reactions of family, friends, and the public. Overall, Caitlyn has been supported at work and did not have the fear that she would lose her job.

Unfortunately, many employees who have revealed their sexual orientation and/or who have identified with a different gender than their biological gender cannot share the same victory in the workplace that Caitlyn experienced. In fact, according to the National LGBTQ Task Force and the National Center for Transgender Equality, the unemployment rate for transgender employees is twice the rate for the general population.[17]

It is becoming more and more evident that LGBTQ employees are falling victim to systemic discrimination in the workplace. Again, part of the reason behind this is organizations' own beliefs about the subject, as we witnessed when Chick-Fil-A's former CEO openly protested same-sex marriage. However, some discrimination and failure to be inclusive results

---

17 National Center for Transgender Equality and the National Gay and Lesbian Task Force. 2009. "National Transgender Discrimination Survey." http://www.thetaskforce.org/static_html/downloads/reports/fact_sheets/transsurvey_prelim_findings.pdf.

from lack of knowledge about the rights and protections that the LGBTQ communities are provided in the workplace.

In 2012, the EEOC made a landmark announcement stating that workplace discrimination and harassment due to a person's sexual orientation and/or gender identity is protected by Title VII of the Civil Rights Act, citing that the Supreme Court has held that "employment actions motivated by gender stereotyping are unlawful sex discrimination."[18]

The Courts Agree!
The 7th Circuit Court of Appeals ruled in April, 2017, that sexual orientation is protected byTitle VII.

Until the Supreme Court rules otherwise, sexual orien-tation will continue to be "of-ficially" a protected class.

However, prior to that announcement, courts were already siding with plaintiffs who brought claims against their employers for discrimination based on sexual orientation and harassment. The landmark case for protection of gender identity in the workplace involved David Schroer, who was living as a male, and who applied, interviewed, and accepted a job offer at the Library of Congress. Subsequent to her accepting the job offer, she informed her new boss that she was transitioning from male to female and preferred to work as a female going forward. After being provided this new information, her job offer was subsequently rescinded by the Library of Congress.

---

18   U.S. Equal Employment Opportunity Commission. "What You Should Know About EEOC and the Enforcement Protections for LGBT Workers." Retrieved from https://www.eeoc.gov/eeoc/newsroom/wysk/enforcement_protections_lgbt_workers.cfm.

The American Civil Liberties Union (ACLU) filed suit on behalf of Schroer and the court agreed that YOU CAN'T DO THAT AT WORK! Schroer was successful in arguing that she had been discriminated against because of her gender. Specifically, the judge stated that employers cannot refuse to hire a candidate just because the candidate, or employee for that matter, "does not conform to the psychological or behavioral stereotypes of his or her birth sex." Additionally, the court opined that sex discrimination includes gender identity.[19]

An employee's freedom to choose which restroom they will use based on their gender identity has been a challenge for organizations over the past year. The EEOC was faced with the opportunity to hear a case involving a transgender employee who was restricted from using the female restroom and was made to use a unisex, single-use restroom called the "executive restroom." The EEOC held that YOU CAN'T DO THAT WORK as the employer's actions were sex-based discrimination under Title VII of the Civil Rights Act. The Commission relied on a case from 2012, in which it made abundantly clear that sex-based discrimination can occur whether he or she is overt or non-overt in his/her transition, or simply because the employer is uncomfortable with the transition. In any case, the employer is constructing a "gender-based" evaluation in violation of Title VII.[20]

Many organizations are now revamping their policies and culture to embrace the LGTBQ community ahead of and more progressively than the requirements of federal and state legislation. According to the 2017 Human Rights Campaign,

---

19 Schroer v. Billington, 577 F. Supp. 2d 293.

20 Lusardi v. John M. McHugh, Secretary, Dept. of the Army, EEOC Appeal No. 0120133395 (Apr. 1, 2015).

517 employers earned 100% on their Corporate Equality Index which measures "leading policies, benefits, and practices for the LGTB workforce and their families."[21] Some additional highlights of the report included:

- 82% of Fortune 500 companies include gender-identity protections in their non-discrimination policies
- 50% of Fortune 500 companies offer transgender-inclusive healthcare coverage
- 387 major businesses have adopted transition guidelines for employees and their teams to establish best practices in transgender inclusion

While these numbers are staggering and a significant improvement to what was reported in previous years, employers in the U.S. are hesitant to embrace this new norm.

I have seen and heard this firsthand as I have coached many HR professionals and organizational leaders on the evolution of workplace rights for transgender employees. Most have told me that their challenge and understanding is not regarding discrimination on the terms and conditions of employment, but more so on how to deal with other employees' reactions to and concerns about their transitioning colleagues.

Here are some tips to help guide you through this new, long overdue, yet complex challenge in the workplace:

---

21   Human Rights Campaign Foundation. 2017. "Corporate Equality Index 2017: Rating Workplaces on Gay, Bisexu-al, and Transgender Equality." http://hrc-assets.s3-website-us-east-1.amazonaws.com//files/assets/resources/CEI-2017-FinalReport.pdf.

- **Open Communication**. Once an employee informs you of his/her gender transition, don't be afraid to ask questions. The better informed you are about their transition, the timeline, and how they would like for their transition to be handled, the better. During this communication, you should also ask the employee *when* he or she would like to be referred to by his or her new gender. Another consideration is to develop a plan with the transitioning employee about how and when to communicate with their peers. When developing this plan, keep in mind that some employees will resist acceptance due to their own religious, political, or moral beliefs and values. It is important to re-emphasize your organization's policy on diversity and inclusion and the importance of treating every employee with respect and dignity.
- **Update Existing Policies and Procedures**. There are several HR policies that may be impacted by having a transgender employee in the workplace, such as your dress code and appearance policies, restroom use policies, and how to change an employee's name and gender for your (recordkeeping) requirements. Additionally, a comprehensive look at your existing benefit offerings should be conducted to ensure that the employee and their qualified dependents are covered according to applicable federal and state laws.
- **Research**. Understand the lingo of gender identity. Not all transitioning employees are coming out as gay. Become familiar with the different ways that people go through this transition, understanding

that there is no cookie-cutter way to transition. Also, be knowledgeable of state and local laws that affect transgender employees.

- **Train and Educate**. Everyone in a leadership role should be trained on this topic to include: communicating with the employee about their transition, how to communicate to co-workers and respond to their reactions, and again re-emphasize your diversity and inclusion policies.
- **Seek Help!** Hire and consult experts on this topic. This can be especially helpful when determining a communication strategy for your existing staff.

As far as restrooms go, many organizations have installed or designated a single-stall, unisex restroom for employees. That is a great idea to address the concerns that some employees may have with sharing a restroom with a transgender employee. Here's the catch: Employers cannot require the transgender employee to use the single-stall, unisex restroom. The restroom must be designated for anyone's use. However, the only way to really address the restroom dilemma is to educate, educate, and re-educate on inclusiveness in the workplace.

Other Implicit Sex-Based Discrimination

Assumption-based sex discrimination is what I call it! Some employers will assume that because a parent has family responsibilities that they may not be able to devote their full attention to their work. As such, they may be overlooked for jobs and promotions or experience other adverse employment actions or treatment. Although being a parent is not explicitly protected under Title VII, the EEOC has acknowledged that parents are being discriminated against in the workplace and have addressed this issue through enforcement guidance on the unlawful treatment of workers with caregiver responsibilities.

In its guidance, the EEOC outlines 10 ways that an employee may establish evidence of unlawful sex-based discrimination.[22]

1.   Whether the employer asked female applicants, but not male applicants, whether they were married or had young children, or about their childcare and other caregiving responsibilities.
2.   Whether decision makers or other officials made stereotypical or derogatory comments about pregnant workers or about working mothers or other female caregivers.
3.   Whether the employer began subjecting the charging party or other women to less favorable treatment soon after it became aware that they were pregnant.
4.   Whether, despite the absence of a decline in work performance, the employer began subjecting the charging party or other women to less favorable treatment after they assumed caregiving responsibilities.
5.   Whether female workers without children or other caregiving responsibilities received more favorable treatment than female caregivers based upon stereotypes of mothers or other female caregivers.

---

22   U.S. Equal Employment Opportunity Commission. 2007. "Enforcement Guidance: Unlawful Disparate Treatment of Workers with Caregiving Responsibilities." https://www.eeoc.gov/policy/docs/caregiving.html.

6.   Whether the employer steered or assigned women with caregiving responsibilities to less prestigious or lower paid positions.
7.   Whether male workers with caregiving responsibilities received more favorable treatment than female workers.
8.   Whether statistical evidence shows disparate treatment against pregnant workers or female caregivers.
9.   Whether the employer deviated from workplace policy when it took the challenged action.
10. Whether the respondent's asserted reason for the challenged action is credible.

These guidelines are applicable to both male and female parents!

The court agrees with the EEOC that it is unlawful for employers to make employment decisions based upon assumptions and stereotypes because of a certain sex. For instance, in one case, a mother of six-year-old triplets and another older child was passed over for a promotion for another less-qualified woman. The mother was able to present evidence of statements from the hiring manager that there was an assumption that she would not be able to balance work responsibility and responsibilities at home, and the court said YOU CAN'T DO THAT AT WORK! What's unique about this case is that although the person that was promoted for the position over the plaintiff was a woman, the court stated that this could still be inferred as sex-based discrimination!

Chapter 4

RELIGIOUS ACCOMMODATIONS

Common mistakes that managers make:

35. Disrespecting employees who have different religious beliefs by not making accommodations for them or refusing to make accommodations for employees' sincere religious beliefs
36. Believing that the only religious "beliefs" that must be accommodated in the workplace are those of "traditional" religions and not sincere moral or ethical beliefs
37. Implementing a rigid dress code which can be viewed as "non-inclusive" or not taking into account the different protected classes of their employees when creating a dress code
38. Using an employee's religious belief as a reason to deny them work
39. Allowing accommodation for all other "personal" related conflicts, but not accommodating for religious observations

We are so fortunate to be living and working in a country that gives us the opportunity to work with people of different ages, race, national origins, cultures, and religion. Having a diverse workforce gives organizations diversity of thought, which can lead to better business results.

However, managing a diverse workforce can also pose many operational challenges for organizations, especially when your workforce is comprised of employees who have different religious observations and practices. Many organizational leaders and human resources departments report that one of their primary challenges comes from attempting to write standard policies and procedures around dress code, scheduling, holidays, celebrations, and or even strategizing day-to-day operations while attempting to accommodate the religious beliefs of their employees.

As stated previously, Title VII of the Civil Rights Act states that an employer must not discriminate against employees (or job applicants) because of their religion. Remember, discrimination can take place when making any decisions on the terms and conditions of employment to include hiring, firing, demotions, promotions, job benefits, pay, and other terms and conditions of employment. That all seems black and white until you get a refusal by two Muslim truck drivers to carry out the duties of their job of transporting alcohol; or when a Jehovah witness refuses to wear a red shirt to a company event to show support of the military; or from a Pentecostal woman who requests to wear a long skirt instead of pants; or others who request to have long beards or hair.

An employee can request a reasonable accommodation based upon their sincere religious beliefs. These beliefs can be not just based upon traditional religions such as Judaism,

Christianity, or the Islamic faith, but can also be based upon an employee's sincere ethical and moral beliefs as well. The examples above are all cases in which employees requested a religious accommodation, but their request was denied by their employer.

So what is an organization's obligation to grant such requests? Employers must grant a request for a religious accommodation unless making such accommodation would pose an undue hardship or burden on the employer's operations. According to the EEOC, undue hardships would include if the accommodation is "costly, compromises workplace safety, decreases workplace efficiency, infringes on the rights of other employees, or requires other employees to do more than their share of potentially hazardous or burdensome work."[23]

In the case in which the two Muslim truck drivers were terminated from their employment when they refused to transport alcoholic beverages due to their sincere religious and moral beliefs, the court concluded that YOU CAN'T DO THAT AT WORK. The court stated that because the trucking company transported items other than alcohol and had allowed drivers to "swap" loads in the past, the two drivers' requests could have been accommodated. Because the swap only burdened the company with a little administrative hassle, it was not a *hardship*.

Most employers include a dress code in their employee handbook. General guidelines may cite business casual, some may say professional. In addition to business casual, and

---

23 U.S. Equal Employment Opportunity Commission. "Religious Garb and Grooming in the Workplace: Rights and Responsibilities." Retrieved from https://www.eeoc.gov/eeoc/publications/qa_religious_garb_grooming. cfm.

professional, employers may add the caveat that the employee's clothes may not be offensive in nature. All those standards are broad and leave room for employees to express their religious expression. However, in some industries, employers can be very specific in regards to dress and/or require that an employee's attire is reflective of the brand of the organization. This is often the case in retail.

Retail organizations have come under scrutiny for dress code policies that attempt to be reflective of their "brand." This was the case with Abercrombie & Fitch, a US-based retailer that targets teenage consumers and had a policy to hire only employees that were reflective of their defined "look": "cool" and "attractive." This criterion ultimately became known as Abercrombie's "look policy." This infamous look policy led to multiple claims of discrimination, to include a 2003 class-action lawsuit that alleged that the retailer preferred to only hire white males for management and its infamous "brand-representative" positions. That class-action lawsuit resulted in a payment of 40 million dollars to impacted applicants. In addition to paying monetary damages for race and gender discrimination claims, Abercrombie also agreed to develop an internal complaint process and create an office of diversity.

Despite these sanctions and alleged improvements, Abercrombie continued to come under legal scrutiny for its look policy, specifically alleging that the retailer's look policy violates employee's rights to religious freedom in the workplace. Just in 2015, the EEOC prevailed in a religious discrimination claim against the retailer when they refused to make an exception to its look policy of banning head coverings and refused to hire a Muslim applicant who wore a hijab, a headscarf that is worn as part of her Muslim faith.[24] This case substantiated the fact that employees should not have to sacrifice their religious beliefs for an opportunity at employment. YOU CAN'T DO THAT AT WORK!

Scheduling

Healthcare and retail are among some other industries that are notorious for operating 24/7 facilities which require an around-the-clock workforce. This poses an exceptional challenge for those employers who have a number of employees who have religious observations that conflict with working after sundown on Fridays and/or on Saturdays or Sundays.

It is customary for a recruiter to ask a candidate if they work during specific shifts on specific days of the week. The recruiter asks this question because they are specifically looking for someone to work during those times and days. If the candidate answers that they cannot, then they are automatically disqualified, right? Well, not necessarily.

This was the case when a Hebrew Israelite candidate applied for a customer service job at a call center in Missouri. When asked if he could work on the weekends, the candidate replied that he could not due to observing the Sabbath from sunup to sundown on Saturdays. The recruiter then replied that the interview was over unless he could work on the weekends. The candidate did not receive the job because of his religious observation and filed a claim with the EEOC. Well, YOU CAN'T DO THAT AT WORK!

---

24   U.S. Equal Employment Opportunity Commission. 2015. "Supreme Court Rules in Favor of EEOC in Abercrombie Religious Discrimination Case." https://www.eeoc.gov/eeoc/newsroom/release/6-1-15.cfm.

The case was settled with a consent decree that included religious harassment and discrimination training for recruiters, a new procedure that allowed for job candidates to ask for a religious accommodation once they received a job offer, and an additional new procedure that allows for job candidates to complete the interview process even if they inform the recruiter of the need for a schedule adjustment. The employer lost the case because it failed to explore possible options to accommodate the job candidate's religious beliefs. In this case, the regional attorney for the EEOC stated that it was not an undue hardship for the employer to provide the employee with an "alternate schedule [when] hundreds of employees [were] available to cover the shift."[25]

Just like with accommodating grooming and dress as discussed before, employers are obligated to accommodate an employee or job candidate's request for a schedule adjustment due to sincerely held religious beliefs unless the request would pose an undue burden for the employer.

Some examples of undue burden (or hardship) include endangering the safety or health of others, violating a seniority system, under-staffing, and significant monetary impact. It is significant to add that the occasional obligation to pay overtime to employees who volunteer to swap days or shifts is not considered an undue burden.

While we're on this subject, I would be remiss if I didn't share a perfect personal example of how a manager can mismanage a religious accommodation request. I was approached by an employee who was also a Baptist minister working in

---

25 U.S. Equal Employment Opportunity Commission. 2012. "Convergys Settles EEOC Suit for Religious Discrimination." https://www.eeoc.gov/eeoc/newsroom/release/2-16-12.cfm.

food services. He had requested Sundays off to attend church services where he was an associate pastor. He was very upset that his request was denied. I knew that the food service department was struggling with staffing on the weekends and instantly and confidently affirmed his manager's decision to deny his request. After hearing that I agreed with the manager's decision, he then informed me that the department was having staffing challenges on weekdays, as well, but that the manager had been accommodating the schedules of college students. Every school term, the manager would adjust their work schedules to accommodate their school schedules. Yet, he had denied the Baptist minister's request to have Sundays off to attend church.

When I contacted the manager to corroborate what I had just learned, he confirmed it, but was insistent that he was doing the right thing. I asked him, "Doesn't it seem strange that we would adjust the schedules of students, who are not in a protected class, and not adjust the schedule of a Baptist preacher who is asking for a religious accommodation?!" The manager replied, "But we are paying for these students' schooling through our tuition reimbursement program, so why wouldn't we support them in their educational pursuits?" I agreed that we should, but also was insistent that we find an accommodation for our Baptist preacher. To accommodate the school schedules of students and not provide a religious accommodation to our Baptist minister citing undue burden was simply unlawful. YOU CAN'T DO THAT AT WORK!

We were able to put together a seamless accommodation with our Baptist minister that worked out for everyone. He had initially been scheduled from 7a-3p on Sundays (during that shift was church hours). He was able to swap with another employee who worked the 3p-11p shift. She was delighted to do the swap as she would now have the opportunity to spend Sunday evenings with her kids and get them prepared for school on Monday. He, too, was pleased as he could attend church service. And they all lived happily ever after!

Not all stories like this end so well. After I resolved this issue, I went on to conduct a comprehensive training with all of the organization's management. Many were surprised about the obligation to accommodate requests for religious accommodations (but ironically had no problems adjusting schedules for school, child care, and other personal requests by employees). Many shared their increased challenges of accommodating schedules, not just due to religious observations, but also for FMLA and ADA accommodations (which we will cover later). I empathized with their concerns, but reiterated that HR is always a resource for helping managers to navigate through religious accommodation requests. I advised that before saying no, managers should always check with us to ensure that there are no options and that granting the accommodation is truly an undue burden.

Practical Tips

- Consider if there are other jobs that the employee may be qualified for that do not require work on the days for which the employee is requesting leave.
- Transfer the employee to another facility that does not operate 24/7.
- Determine if other employees are willing to swap or switch work schedules. However, with this solution

you may run afoul of having to pay the switched employee overtime.

Accommodating religious practices and observations can admittedly be burdensome and overwhelming for some employers. However, if your policies and practices are too restrictive, insensitive, and under-inclusive, you should probably know that YOU CAN'T DO THAT AT WORK!

Chapter 5

AGE DISCRIMINATION IN EMPLOYMENT ACT

Common mistakes that managers make:

40. Focusing on one generation for the future of work
41. Advertising for positions by using language such as "new grad" or "college student"
42. Trying to save money by laying off high-salary employees but not taking into account their age and experience
43. Creating internship or apprenticeship programs which are under-inclusive

Not a day goes by that my LinkedIn timeline, Twitter, or blogs that I subscribe to are not flooded with articles and blogs on how to manage this unprecedented multi-generational workforce. However, the majority of these articles address one generation and one generation alone, the millennials. There is certainly reason for there to be focus on recruitment, retention, performance management, and recognizing millenniums in the workforce. However, what HR leaders are forgetting are the other generations.

Under the Age Discrimination in Employment Act (ADEA), employees and applicants 40 and over are protected from discrimination in the terms and conditions of employment. The older you are, the more protected you are in the workplace.

As an example, let's say that there are two applicants for one job. One is 45, the other is 65. Unlike the criteria for proving a Title VII discrimination claim, if the 45-year-old is selected for the job, the 65-year-old can still claim age discrimination although the 45-year-old is in the same protected class. Many argue that the 40 threshold is too low for today's work environment. Perhaps they are correct as the workforce today looks quite different than the workforce of 1967.

Employees are remaining in the workforce longer today than in 1967 when the ADEA was passed. There are many contributing factors to the longevity of today's workforce. First, the recession of 2008 caused many who were due to retire to delay their retirement and many who were retired to re-enter the workforce. Additionally, changes to social security programs delayed the retirement age, since retirees now receive increased benefits the longer they wait for retirement up to age 70. Moreover, many employers transitioned from defined retirement benefits plans to less certain 401(k) plans. Other factors that have increased longevity in the workforce include longer life expectancy, the availability of less physically strenuous work, and the decline of attractive health care coverage for retirees. This has created an unprecedented challenge for employers as they now have to plan their workforce strategies for five generations of workers. However, many organizations have failed to nail how to accomplish this and have instead opted to just focus on recruiting and retaining young talent.

Hollywood has even taken notice of the shifting dynamics of the workforce with the focus on a younger, seemingly fast-paced, more productive generation. There are movies like *The*

Internship, which features two laid-off salesmen who apply for and are accepted to an internship at Google. They are also the only non-college-aged interns. The movie highlights the obstacles that one might face working for a company that is set up to attract and retain millennial employees, from Skype interviewing to playing ping pong at work.

The Intern, starring Robert DeNiro, also captured the challenges of the multigenerational workforce as *The Internship,* when a baby-boomer is hired for an internship for an online retailer and is not initially embraced by the company's CEO. Eventually, the older worker wins the CEO's respect as he is able to offer much-needed advice and mentorship that helps her to make some life-changing decisions both at home and at work.

The reality, however, is no laughing matter. Mark Zuckerberg, the CEO of Facebook, said famously at a 2007 conference that "young people are just smarter." Unfortunately, Facebook is not the only organization that shares his sentiments. As recently as 2015, organizations such as Electronic Arts, Dropbox, Apple, and Yahoo all listed "new grad" as a preference in job postings. Although it can be argued that the average age of new college grads is rising, I think we can all agree on the inference. In response to the blatant discriminatory inference of using language such as "recent college graduate," "college student," and/or "young blood," organizations in the tech industry have replaced those terms with less obvious terms such as "digital native." In 2014, the EEOC reported that out of the 121 alleged discriminatory advertising practices, 111 of them were alleged to be unlawful due to age discrimination, also known as ageism.

Recently, it has been alleged that ageism has been "built right into the software" of online job search websites such as Indeed.com and Careerbuilder.com.[26] The allegations are that applicants are forced to select from a drop-down menu of options, such as "years attended college" that have dates that do not go back far enough for older applicants to complete. Some sites did not give the option to go back just as early as 1980, which would bar anyone over the age of 52 from completing applications!

The EEOC has been able to settle and win ADEA suits where employers have disproportionally and unlawfully laid off older workers because of their age. Some examples of unlawful age discrimination include when one employer incentivizes its employees to retire by age 55 by providing a "cliff." This benefit was not offered if their employees retired after 55. Additionally, it was found to be unlawful for an employer to require older employees to make higher pension contributions than younger employees. A law firm learned this lesson the hard way when it forced its older workers to retire. The EEOC successfully challenged this and settled with the firm for a whopping 27.5 million dollars that was paid out to 32 impacted partners. Other examples of age-based discrimination include reducing the accrual rate of paid time off for older workers. The EEOC has said that is outright, intentional discrimination against older workers. YOU CAN'T DO THAT AT WORK!

Many organizations will argue that older workers who have remained with the same company for several years and receive high salaries work at a much slower pace and are less productive. But nothing could be further from the truth.

---

26 CNBC. 2010. "Online Job Sites May Block Older Workers." http://www.cnbc.com/2017/03/10/online-job-sites-may-block-older-workers.html?__source=yahoo%7Cfinance%7Cheadline%7Cheadline%7Cstory&par=yahoo&doc=104331969&yptr=yahoo.

A diverse workforce that includes older employees brings diversity of thought, creativity, and innovation. Instead of thinking of ways to push older workers out of the workplace, organizations should focus on ways to leverage them.

To avoid legal liability, and also to maintain a multi-generational workforce, employers should look for creative ways to leverage the value that employees of all ages bring to the workforce.

- **Expanded Apprentice and Internship Programs:** Maybe Hollywood got it right. Internships should not be limited to those who are enrolled in college or are "college age."
- **Start a Returnship Program:** Companies such as Goldman Sachs, Centrica PLC, Capital One, and MetLife all have returnship programs. Like the character played by Robert De Niro in the Intern, a returnship program gives retired and other people who have been out of the workforce for a while the opportunity to return to the workforce through an internship program. The program exposes the potential employee to the opportunity to "try out" the company and the position while also giving the company an opportunity to see the value the potential employee would bring to their organization. Just like a typical internship, except this won't be their first rodeo!
- **Cross-Generational Mentorships:** Many younger employees don't know the value of working with a seasoned employee until they've had the opportunity to just sit down and shoot the "you know what" with

them! Seasoned employees have been around the block a time or two and have so many experiences to share. Experience is the best teacher in life. In return, seasoned employees will also be surprised to discover what they can learn from younger workers. "There's an app for that?!" Create an opportunity for cross-generational, non-work related conversation. You'll be surprised at the results.

Whether you are a traditionalist, baby-boomer, gen x, gen y, or gen z, we are all in the workforce and here to stay! And if organizations think they can just shun one generation for another, well think again, because YOU CAN'T DO THAT AT WORK!

Chapter 6

REVERSE DISCRIMINATION - DOES IT REALLY EXIST?

Common mistakes managers make:

44.   Creating an affirmative action plan that is not a result of historical discrimination
45.   Having diversity initiatives which in turn discriminate against those outside the targeted protected class

As I stated earlier in this section, some people are unaware of their rights in the workplace and have often falsely believed that they have no protections. When they realize that their organization is promoting efforts to drive diversity, they are oftentimes under the false presumption that they are experiencing reverse discrimination, meaning that they won't have access to equal employment opportunity because it is being given to someone outside of their protected class who is less qualified. This leads to the presumption that they are the victim of reverse discrimination in the workplace.

If I've said it once, I have no problem repeating it: A diverse workforce brings diversity of thought, which leads to organizational success. Many organizations' talent-management strategies have long included having policies and procedures in place that mitigate the need to establish formal diversity programs.

It seems like it would be easy, right? Recruit from diverse colleges, advertise job openings in diverse areas, and hire candidates based solely on their background, education, and experience regardless of their membership in a protected class and the result will be a diverse workforce. This is easier said than done for some organizations that have been around for a while and have inadvertently established a practice of institutional discrimination. Institutional discrimination occurs when an organization has had a history of hiring and promoting employees with an unconscious or unintentional bias.

Although Title VII was passed over 50 years ago, some industries still struggle to maintain a workforce that is reflective of the demographic in their geographic area. This is not only true in areas such as the legal field, where it known that there is an opportunity for diversity, but also in modern day industries such as computer coding. As such, some organizations have acknowledged their lack of diversity and adopted diversity goals and initiatives to remedy the effects of historical discrimination. Others have adopted diversity goals and initiatives not to remedy historical discrimination, but to facilitate their desire for their workforce to be reflective of the surrounding demographics and customer base. The distinction between the two objectives could possibly answer whether or not organizations' diversity initiatives are lawful or could result in reverse discrimination allegations.

Can an organization require vendors to become more diverse? Walmart thinks so!

In 2006, Walmart Stores, Inc. shocked the legal community when it acknowledged and addressed the lack of minorities and women in some of the nation's largest law firms and cut ties with two of them because of their lack of diversity.

For the remaining firms, Mr. Sam Reeves, Senior Vice-President and General Counsel, required them to submit 3-5 names of lawyers who would serve as "relationship partners" with Walmart's legal department with at least one woman and one minority on the list.

Rosiland Brewer, the first woman and African-American to lead a WalMart division entity, received both applause and backlash when she recalled a meeting with a supplier and noted that other side of table was all Caucasian males. She reiterated her commitment to diversity among her team and also expects it of her suppliers.

The EEOC supports the adoption of diversity initiatives and affirmative action plans if they provide for race- and gender-conscious actions in its Affirmative Action Guidelines. These voluntary efforts must be established to recognize the effects of past or present discriminatory employment practices. An employer may determine that their past employment practices may have been unintentionally discriminatory by conducting a reasonable self-analysis of such practices.

The Supreme Court has not explicitly confirmed that an employer can consider a person's protected class when making employment decisions as part of a diversity program, but has said that while "Title VII does prohibit taking a person's protected class into consideration when making employment decisions, affirmative action plans are designed to eliminate conspicuous racial imbalance in traditionally segregated job categories."[27] In addition to the criteria of addressing imbalances of traditionally segregated job categories, the court has also provided additional guidelines:

- The plan should not absolutely bar the advancement of employees in protected categories that are not targeted.
- The plan should be temporary to address the imbalance.[28]
- After a New Jersey school board considered race when laying off equally qualified teachers, the lower courts held that its affirmative action plan was not premised on remedying historical institutional discrimination. The school board's plan was to maintain a diverse staff despite the layoffs rather than eradicating the historical effects of discrimination. YOU CAN'T DO THAT AT WORK!

Practical Considerations

Employers can still implement diversity initiatives to both remedy the effects of past institutional discrimination and also in an effort to maintain a diverse workforce with these practical tips.

---

27 United Steelworkers v. Weber, 443 U.S. 193 (1979).
28 Johnson v. Transportation Agency, Santa Clara County 480 U.S. 616 (1987).

- Achieve hiring of diverse candidates by recruiting from diverse communities, colleges, social media, and ethnic or female-centric professional organizations.
- Ensure that everyone in your current organization is being developed equally and is educated on career pathing within your organization.
- Avoid tying diversity goals to incentives for hiring managers as it is still unclear that when two candidates are equal in qualifications and the manager selects the minority candidate to fulfill diversity goals, if this is lawful conduct.
- Hire the best candidate!! Cannot say it enough. Federal anti-discrimination statutes protect EVERYONE in the workplace.

PART II

HEALTH AND
WELLNESS AT WORK

Chapter 7

AMERICANS WITH DISABILITIES ACT

Common mistakes that managers make:

---

46. Not understanding that not all disabilities are visible

47. Not knowing that a person who may not have a substantially limiting disability now, but did in the past, may still be a person with a disability under the Americans with Disabilities Act (ADA)

48. Thinking that employees have to use the verbiage "reasonable accommodation" when requesting one

49. Summarily denying a reasonable accommodation request without engaging in the interactive process

50. Not realizing that unless it poses undue hardship, you must grant a reasonable accommodation

51. Not knowing that job applicants are afforded the same protection under the ADA as employees of an organization

Health and Wellness at Work

Without a doubt, more and more employers are realizing that employees would take opportunities for workplace flexibility over an increase in pay. Workplace flexibility not only allows employees to better achieve work-life balance, but it has also been proven that employees who are given the opportunity to work from home actually are more productive. Caregivers especially enjoy this option simply because it gives you back hours in the day when you subtract just commuting time alone (not to mention the saved time of getting dressed if you opt to work in your PJs)!

Early in 2013, Yahoo! CEO Marrisa Mayer rocked the tech industry when she banned her employees from the option of working remotely. The decision impacted many working parents who utilized this option to help them balance career and parenthood. Mayer complicated the matter more when she announced that she was six months pregnant and built her very own nursery for her baby right in her Yahoo! office. Because Mayer was CEO of the company and had not only the authority, but the money to do so, she was not faced with the same challenges that most people face when attempting to work while being a caregiver.

Despite most everyone's attempt to be their most present and engaged person at work, there are oftentimes unforeseeable extenuating circumstances that might mitigate our efforts to do so. Even if we put forth our very best effort to remain well, we cannot guarantee the same for our children, our spouses, or our parents. Unexpected illnesses that could potentially affect our ability to work are bound to happen sometimes in our career, as is the expectation that we bring children into this world. But, shouldn't everyone be afforded the same opportunity that Marissa Mayer had – the ability to care for the health and well-being of yourself and your loved ones without sacrificing our careers? The answer is yes!

I was born with a congenital heart defect that resulted in me spending most of my childhood in hospitals. At the age of 11 years old, I underwent open heart surgery. Not to give away my age, but my childhood medical issues occurred before any laws were passed that would have protected my parents' jobs when they cared for me. But they were lucky. I had two sets of grandparents, two great-grandmothers, and many of aunts and uncles and church members who assisted them with my care. Additionally, they were educators so they had a couple of months during the year when they did not have to worry about their job security while caring for their sick child. Not everyone has that support system or flexibility.

A few years ago, I found out that my father, who was located hundreds of miles away from me, had been placed in hospice care the day after I had accepted a new job. When I called my new boss to share the news, she understood and allowed me to postpone my start date by a week so that I could spend some final days with my father. However, because I was not eligible for any job-protected leaves due to being just hired, I never saw my father alive again.

The laws that will be discussed in this section will be applicable to 99.9% of employees (even CEOs). While arguably hard to manage administratively and sometimes abused by some, these laws should be viewed favorably for both employers and employees. Employees can take care of their own health and well-being without fear of losing their jobs and employers should not want employees at work who are too sick to be there or are unproductive and disengaged because they are thinking about who is going to care for their sick loved ones.

The reality is that many managers view the use of leave and disability laws by their employees as a way to avoid working, a way to avoid time and attendance issues, and a burden on business operations. While I can say that it is indisputable that some employees do abuse leave and disability laws, that is usually not the case. But as they say, one bad apple (or experience in this case) can spoil the bunch! In my experience, I hear the same complaints from managers time and time again:

- Employees use leave and disability laws to avoid disciplinary action for time and attendance issues
- Employees use job-protected leave time when denied vacation time
- Employees are on job-protected leave but are working another job or are on social media having a good time
- I don't know how to accommodate an employee's disability accommodation request
- I don't know how to track intermittent leave time

Sound familiar? Shall I say more?! This section will explore the various laws and protections that are afforded to employees when they or their families are faced with a serious medical condition, disability, and/or are expecting to bring life into this world. This section will also discuss how to manage job-protected leaves, disability accommodation requests, as well as how to legally handle suspicions of abuse. Additionally, this section will cover how using an employee's genetic information in hiring decisions and/or as part of a wellness program could potentially violate federal law.

The Americans with Disabilities Act (ADA)

In my opinion, one of the most challenging workplace anti-discrimination laws to navigate through is the ADA, which prohibits employment discrimination against qualified individuals with disabilities. Remember, everyone is in a protected class, right? Most protected classes are obvious to employers, thus making it easy to avoid discrimination.

However, employees with disabilities may not be as obvious. Moreover, an employee's disability status can change in the blink of the eye. The applications of the ADA are very broad and situation specific. To further complicate things, in 2008, Congress amended the ADA to broaden its definition of "disability" and removed the "extensive analysis" that the court had to navigate through previously to determine if an employee was in fact disabled. These changes have added additional headaches for organizations as they attempt to comply with this law.

The EEOC has been aggressive with holding employers accountable for failing to accommodate disabled employees in ways that have been unprecedented. If your organization has policies that have caps for the amount of time an employee can take leave or "no-fault" attendance policies, pay very close attention to this section!

When a Disability Isn't Visible

It can be difficult for managers to manage mental disabilities in the workplace for many reasons, including: the employee may be embarrassed to share the details about their mental disability and/or the manager may not know how to approach an employee about a perceived mental disability.

The EEOC has recognized the number of employees suffering from depression, post-traumatic stress disorder (PTSD), bi-polar disorder, and other mental conditions and has issued some guidelines for employers to help them to mitigate claims of discrimination and harassment and tips for making reasonable accommodations.

In addition to providing caution to employers about discriminating against employees with mental health conditions, it also provides caution about myths and stereotypes about mental and health-related conditions and cautions about when an employer can ask medical-related questions (only in four situations).

The guidance also offers reasonable accommodation recommendations in these in-stances:
- Altered breaks and modified schedules
- Specific shift assignments
- Quiet office space
- Telecommuting

A qualified individual with a disability is defined as "an individual with a disability who, with or without reasonable accommodation, can perform the essential functions of the employment position that such individual holds or desires." The ADA states that a disability is:

- With a physical or mental impairment that substantially limits one or more major life activity of such individuals
- With a record of such impairment
- Who are regarded as having such impairment, but who are able to perform the essential functions of the job with or without a reasonable accommodation

After reading those three bullet points, you probably have no better understanding of what constitutes a qualified individual under the ADA than before. You're not alone in your confusion. Let's explore some examples:

Obesity, carpel tunnel disease, stuttering, and depression have all been considered physical and mental impairments that substantially limit a major life activity. Examples of major life activities include: walking, talking, standing, sitting, seeing, hearing, and yes, even working. In one case, a court even cited "major cell growth" is a major life activity deeming a breast cancer survivor in remission as disabled.

A person who may not have a substantially limiting condition now, but had one in the past, may be a person with a disability. This explains the second prong of the analysis: a record of such impairment. An example that the EEOC gives here is that an employee is *perceived* as having a learning disability but does not.

Although a person may deem to have a disability, they must still be able to complete the essential functions of the job that they are applying for or currently hold. According to the EEOC, when determining essential job functions, these are factors to be considered:

- the employer's assessment of which functions are essential, as demonstrated by job descriptions written before the employer posts or advertises for the position
- whether the position exists to perform that function
- the experience of employees who actually hold that position
- the time spent performing the function
- the consequences of not performing the function
- whether other employees are available to perform the function, and
- the degree of expertise or skill required to perform the function.

Essential job functions may change throughout the course of an employee's tenure in a position which may deem an employee unable to work due to his/her disability. This was the case when a court reporter specialist was assigned to one control room and was able to manage her incontinence. However, her position was eventually abolished and she was required to rotate through all of the court and control rooms as other court reporters did. In response, the employee requested to be assigned to one court or control room as a reasonable accommodation and was denied her request.

The court sided with the employer on this one, stating that the employer had the right to restructure the court reporting jobs to evenly distribute the workload and recreate an essential function that required the ability to rotate.[29]

Again, employees can request reasonable accommodation to their job duties, assignments, shifts, and other conditions of employment due to their disability. A reasonable accommodation request made by an employee does not have to be in plain English and does not have to use the verbiage "reasonable accommodation." An example that the EEOC gives is "an employee tells her supervisor, 'I'm having trouble getting to work at my scheduled starting time because of medical treatments I'm undergoing.'" This is a request for a reasonable accommodation. Once an employer is on notice that an employee is requesting a reasonable accommodation, they must then engage in the interactive process with the employee.

The interactive process allows employers to determine the needs of the employee and what accommodation options are available to them. The interactive process can include asking for medical documentation describing the disability and functional limitations. It is important to note that an employer should not ask for medical documentation if the disability is obvious (employee is paralyzed and in a wheelchair) or if they have already provided sufficient evidence.

As a practical consideration, here are 5 ways that you can accommodate employees with a disability:

ACCOMMODATION	DESCRIPTION
Modified Schedule/Part-Time Work	Adjust arrival and departure time Allow for periodic breaks Condense work schedule

---

[29]   Gratzl v. Office of the Chief Judges, 601 F.3d 674 (7th Cir. 2010).

Leave	Allow employee to use paid/unpaid leave
Job Restructuring	Alter how the employee performs his/her work Reallocate or redistribute how employee's work is performed
Modify Work Policies	Dress code policies Eating at workstation policies Break policies Attendance policies Job transfer policies
Reassignment	Reassign to vacant position

An employer must accommodate an employee's request for a reasonable accommodation unless granting the request poses an undue hardship on the organization. While there are no hard-and-fast rules on what constitutes undue hardship, the EEOC does give some guidance:[30]

- The nature and cost of the accommodation needed
- The overall financial resources of the facility making the reasonable accommodation, the number of persons employed at this facility, and the effect on expenses and resources of the facility
- The overall financial resources, size, number of employees, and type and location of facilities

---

30 U.S. Equal Employment Opportunities Commission. "Requesting Reasonable Accommodation." Retrieved from https://www.eeoc.gov/policy/docs/accommodation.html#requesting.

of the employer (if the facility involved in the reasonable accommodation is part of a larger entity)
- The type of operation of the employer, including the structure and functions of the workforce, the geographic separateness, and the administrative or fiscal relationship of the facility involved in making the accommodation to the employer
- The impact of the accommodation on the operation of the facility

The clear lesson learned from this guidance is that the EEOC and the courts look at the total picture and operation of the organization. The more available resources and human capital an organization has, the more difficult it is to prove undue hardship.

A case that illustrates an employer's obligation under the ADA to engage in the interactive process was when a medical resident was having serious problems communicating with fellow colleagues and patients in a professional manner. His employer suspected that he suffered from Asperger's Syndrome and referred him for examination, which confirmed their suspicions. The employee continued to have issues related to job performance and was ultimately fired.

Subsequent to his termination, the employee requested as a reasonable accommodation "knowledge and understanding" about his condition, that his colleagues be informed about his medical condition, and finally that he self-educate and remedy his performance deficiencies. The hospital was unable to grant his request for this accommodation due to a lack of resources, but was able to offer him another residency position in pathology, which would require little to no patient communication, thus denying his required accommodation.

The court agreed with the employer's determination that the employee's accommodation request would pose an undue hardship. This case highlights a good faith attempt by an employer to engage in the interactive process with the employee by listening to his proposed accommodations, communicating the challenges of implementing his proposition (demonstrating undue hardship) and offering alternative, reasonable solutions.

Job applicants are afforded the same protections under the ADA as employees of an organization. A job applicant may even ask for a reasonable accommodation to assist them through the hiring process. An employer may ask an applicant if they require a reasonable accommodation to complete specific job functions only if they have an obvious disability. Otherwise, those questions should be reserved until after a conditional job offer has been extended. Questions regarding reasonable accommodations after a conditional job offer has been made should be asked of all applicants, not just those with obvious or perceived disabilities.

Chapter 8

THE PREGNANCY DISCRIMINATION ACT

Common mistakes that managers make:

---

52. Not knowing that the Pregnancy Discrimination Act (PDA) also covers conditions related to past pregnancies as well as intended and future pregnancies
53. Forcing pregnant employees to take leave even if they are still able to work
54. Not accommodating lactating and breastfeeding employees
55. Offering light-duty assignments to other employees, but not pregnant employees

The Pregnancy Discrimination Act (PDA)

The Pregnancy Discrimination Act (PDA) is an amendment to Title VII which prohibits employers from discriminating against women employees and applicants because they are pregnant, are affected by pregnancy-related conditions, or are affected by recent childbirth. Additionally, the act covers past pregnancies and intended or potential pregnancies (reproductive risk, infertility treatment, use of contraception, and abortion). The Pregnancy Discrimination Act may seem cut and dried, but it can pose some complex challenges for employers. For instance:

1.   Employers can't force employees to take leave from work if they are still able to complete their job functions.
2.   Lactation and breastfeeding are viewed by the EEOC as pregnancy-related medical conditions that need to be accommodated.
3.   Parental policies must be the same for men and women. Parental leave is different than a medical leave that may be needed due to giving birth or recovering from childbirth.

While the pregnancy itself is not considered a disability under the ADA, pregnancy-related complications do fall under the ADA. This leads me to discuss one of the primary challenges of navigating the Pregnancy Discrimination Act, which is when an employee informs her employer that she can no longer perform all or some of her job due to her pregnancy (or conditions related to it). The Supreme Court recently heard a case that involved a pregnant UPS worker who was refused an accommodation for either light duty or a return as a truck driver without having to lift boxes, since her medical provider had advised her against lifting more than 20 pounds.[31] UPS summarily denied her request, stating that they only offered light duty according to three conditions: for employees who are injured on the job, employees covered under the ADA, and

---

31   Young v. United Parcel Service, Inc., 135 S.Ct. 1338.

to employees who had lost Department of Transportation certification because of physical ailments like sleep apnea. They did not offer light duty to pregnant employees. They then required the pregnant employee to go on an extended medical leave since she could not carry out her current duties.

UPS argued that it did not violate the PDA as she did not fall into one of the three categories (remember pregnancy itself is not a disability) and that it had a pregnancy-neutral policy, meaning UPS considers pregnancy the same way they would an off-the-job injury that garners no special treatment. The employee argued that the PDA should be interpreted such that as long as an employer accommodates some employees with disabilities, pregnant workers who are similarly unable to work must receive the same treatment.

It can be argued that UPS's policy is inconsistent with the EEOC's guidance on accommodating pregnant employees.[32] In its 2014 guidance on pregnancy discrimination, it states that if employers offer temporary light-duty work to non-pregnant employees, it must offer the same to pregnant employees with the same restrictions regardless even if they are not considered "disabled" under the ADA.

Can you do that at work? The Supreme Court did not rule one way or the other on this case, but rather sent the case back down to the circuit court. But what the court did say was if an employer refused to accommodate a pregnant employee while accommodating other (non-pregnant) employees "similar in their ability or inability to work," the employer must have a "legitimate, non-discriminatory reason" for doing so.

---

32 U.S. Equal Employment Opportunities Commission. "Enforcement Guidelines and Related Documents." Retrieved from https://www.eeoc.gov/laws/guidance/enforcement_guidance.cfm.

UPS has since changed its "pregnancy-neutral" policy and now offers pregnant employees light duty if needed. However, they still maintain that their change of heart was on their own accord and not required under the PDA. We will keep an eye on the revelations of this case as it is sure to set precedence for PDA.

Practical Tips

- Avoid determining reasonable accommodation based upon how that accommodation would impact the morale of other employees.
- Designate a person or department within your organization who handles requests for reasonable accommodations to ensure consistency, thus mitigating legal liability.
- Engage in the interactive process by providing alternative accommodation if the original request cannot be accommodated.
- Keep records of all accommodation requests and medical information obtained for such in a separate, confidential file.
- Train all managers on not only your duty to accommodate, but also on your policies for handling such requests.

Chapter 9

THE FAMILY MEDICAL LEAVE ACT

Common mistakes that managers make:

56. Thinking that employees have to be bedridden while on Family Medical Leave (FMLA)
57. Thinking that employees can't moonlight while on an FMLA leave
58. Confusing short-term disability benefits with FMLA protections
59. Not knowing that if an employee requests an extended leave after they have exhausted FMLA, it must be analyzed as an ADA accommodation
60. Not accommodating an employee's disability accommodation because of the impact it will have on the morale of other employees
61. Having an automatic termination policy after an employee has exhausted their job - protected FMLA leave
62. Not knowing that you can investigate and take action against FMLA abuse
63. Not knowing that the Uniform Services Employment and Reemployment Act adds on an extra layer of

protection in the workplace for employees in the military

64. Not knowing that you must hold a position for a person on military leave for 5 years and the employee must be returned to the same or similar position

65. Not knowing that employees returning from military leave are entitled to the pay increases they would have received had they never left

66. Not knowing that a service member's spouse, parent, or child is entitled to Qualified Exigency leave under the FMLA

The Family Medical Leave Act

If I had a penny for every time a manager came running into my office waving a posting from the social media account of an employee who was out on a job-protected FMLA leave, I would not be writing this book, but rather vacationing on a private island off the coast of France!

In the post, the employee would be relaxing on a sandy beach, sipping a cocktail and smiling at the camera with the caption, "My home for the next twelve weeks!" We've all been there, and we've all been ready to call that employee's house and fire them. The truth of the matter is that here we are at work struggling to fill their shift and listening to our employee's gripes and moans about them being on leave and not really being "sick." So, once their colleague sees that photo, they can't wait to bring it your attention and stand with their arms folded waiting for your reaction.

So what *can* we do?

Believe it or not, maybe nothing. It all depends on what that employee's serious medical condition is under the FMLA. The Family Medical Leave Act gives eligible employees up to 12 weeks, unpaid, job-protected leave if they have a serious medical condition that makes them unable to perform the functions of their job or:

- For the birth and care of the newborn child of an employee;
- For placement with the employee of a child for adoption or foster care;
- To care for an immediate family member (spouse, child, or parent) with a serious health condition; or
- To take medical leave when the employee is unable to work because of a serious health condition.

Who is an eligible employee?

- Must have worked for 1,250 hours in the previous 12 months.

Oftentimes, when a manager thinks "serious medical condition," they picture their employees laid up in bed, unable to leave the house (and surely unable to go to the beach). A serious medical condition is an illness, injury, impairment, or physical or mental condition that involves *inpatient care* (defined as an overnight stay in a hospital, hospice, or residential medical care facility; any overnight admission to such facilities is an automatic trigger for FMLA eligibility) or *continuing treatment* by a health care provider. In this particular example, the employee at the beach may have a serious medical condition that incapacitates them from going to work for more than three consecutive days and requires ongoing medical treatment or a single treatment with prescription medication.

Still confused about how she is able to go to the beach and get away with it?

Consider this. Our beach-going employee is a nurse. She was recently diagnosed with plantar fasciitis, a condition that involves pain and inflammation throughout the bottom of your foot. This is a common condition among workers who constantly stand on their feet – teachers, nurses, and factory workers. Her doctor has recommended she stays off her feet, undergo physical therapy four days a week for twelve weeks, and take medicine for pain. She is doing just that. She has been diagnosed with a serious medical condition as defined by the FMLA and is following her doctor's orders.

There is nothing in the act that states where and how you recover. Additionally, the employee cannot perform the functions, as her job that requires her to stand all day on her feet. She could go to the beach, be at her house, or at the movies. It does not matter where she is as long as she stays off of her feet and goes to physical therapy as the doctor has instructed. No laws have been broken.

It is understood that when employees choose to boast about not being at work when they are on an approved, job-protected medical leave, that puts you in a very awkward predicament because now you feel that you owe the employees who saw the post an explanation for your inaction. But the truth of the matter is, you do not. A good response is a simple, "Thank you for bringing this to my attention. We will investigate and respond accordingly; however, we cannot discuss with you the outcome of the investigation." More likely than not, your employees will continue to gripe and complain, especially if the social media posts continue, but you simply cannot engage in any conversation with them regarding your employee on leave. What you can do is to provide them with the support and resources they need while you are short on staff. Consider hiring a temporary employee or transferring someone in from another department. These options are not always doable, but communication and appreciation for them stepping up to fill in is imperative.

On FMLA Leave, but Working Somewhere Else

What if your employee who is out on an approved, job-protected leave is not at the beach resting their achy foot, but is in fact working somewhere else! Surely we can fire them for that, right?!

Wrong! Well, it depends.

I am originally from the South, and once lived in a state where both selling and firing off firecrackers is a huge deal. I mean HUGE. I worked as a human resources manager at a manufacturing facility where again, almost all the jobs required employees to stand on their feet for most, if not all, of their working time.

One employee who was on an approved, job-protected leave was spotted on the side of the road sitting under a tent selling fireworks. That sighting sent the plant manager into a flying rage of fire. He walked into my office with his termination paperwork already signed, sealed, and ready to be delivered. Once he explained to me what he had seen, I simply tore the paperwork in half and threw it in the trash.

Like our beach resting, foot-aching employee from before, he, too, had a serious medical condition that infringed on his ability to stand on his feet. Although he was not able to work at the plant, he could work at the fireworks stand or any other second job as long as the physical demands are different than what his physical limitations are as outlined by his medical condition.

Although the FMLA does not prohibit working a second job while on FMLA, it does not prohibit organizations from doing so. If an organization has a policy in place that restricts working other employment (moonlighting) while on a paid and/or unpaid leave, then it can forbid the employee from working a second job while on FMLA leave. However, these policies must have already been in place and apply to all leaves, not just FMLA leave. Additionally, the Family Medical Leave Act does not require that employers pay their employees while out on leave, but many employers provide short-term disability insurance that may cover any lost wages from missed work.

Whether or not an employee can collect short-term disability (STD) and work at another job is strictly based on your company policy or the terms and conditions of your short-term disability insurance carrier. The same applies if you allow your employees to utilize accrued sick time while on leave. Because federal law does not require either STD or paid sick leave, it is strictly left to employers to address such issues in their policies.

Restricted Duty

So, you're probably thinking, "I have plenty of work that beach relaxer with the achy foot or fireworks-selling manufacturing worker can be doing other than standing on their feet all day. Can't I make them come in and file some paperwork or something?"

You are most certainly welcome to offer the employee restricted or alternative duty if they have physical limitations, but according to the FMLA, an employee does not have to accept your offer. If an employee is eligible for paid short-term benefits as explained above, they likely will decline your offer and recover at home (or the beach or the fireworks stand). However, if an employee is not entitled to short-term disability benefits, or has no paid sick or vacation time, they may accept your offer so that they will not lose any pay.

We will not cover workers' compensation laws in detail in this book as workers' comp is regulated by state laws. However, I would like to note that if you offer transitional or restricted duty to employees who are out on a workers' compensation leave, they must accept the offer.

FMLA/ADA

Oh, what a tangled web we weave when we think employees are job protected for only twelve weeks! Up until about two years ago, employers were safe to have hard-and-fast leave policies that stated if an employee remained out on an FMLA leave for longer than twelve consecutive weeks, their jobs would be automatically backfilled, or even worse, they would automatically be terminated.

It was also safe to have policies that capped intermittent leave to 480 hours. Well, YOU CAN'T DO THAT AT WORK.

Let's revisit our beach-going-achy-foot nurse. Despite going to physical therapy for twelve weeks and receiving regular cortisone shots, she is still in lots of pain and her doctor has recommended surgery — hence she will need more than twelve weeks of FMLA leave. That is probably the last thing you want to hear as a manager, as you have been looking forward to either her return or the ability to backfill her position so that you can return to your normal staffing status. However, you no longer have the ability to pull the trigger so quickly.

The EEOC and recent court decisions have determined that an employee's request for extended leave past the statutory twelve-week period must be considered a reasonable accommodation under the ADA. As discussed in Chapter 7, under the ADA, employers must now engage in the interactive process with the employee to determine if they can grant her request for extended leave, as a reasonable accommodation, or determine if there are other reasonable accommodations other than offering more leave time.

Other reasonable accommodations, as previously mentioned, could come in the form of a modified work duty assignment. Perhaps she could conduct post-discharge phone calls, or conduct one-to-one patient observations? If those types of accommodations or other modified duty assignments which do not require her to stand on her feet are available, then I suggest you offer those to her in lieu of extending her leave. In fact, because she has now exhausted her FMLA, job-protected leave, she now has to accept the reasonable accommodation being offered to her so long as it is effective. What is essential is that the employer engages with the employee to understand the nature of her disability and limitations, while exploring and discussing all options with the employee.

It is important to note that when the employee requests an additional leave past her original 12 weeks, she does not have to state specifically that she is requesting an accommodation under the ADA. It is up to you as her employer to determine that she has a physical impairment that substantially limits or restricts a major life activity – in this case, working.

If the employer cannot provide the employee with alternative duty assignments, then the employer must consider granting the employee's request for an extended leave. If the employer believes that extending the employee's leave is not an option, they must demonstrate that by determining whether or not granting the employee an extended leave as a reasonable accommodation will cause undue hardship.

Proving undue hardship can be difficult to demonstrate, and there are no hard-and-fast rules that apply. Many employers mistake undue hardship for simply meaning that the accommodation request would pose only a financial burden on the organization. Proving undue hardship can be any reasonable accommodation request that would significantly alter the fundamental nature of the business. For our beach-resting-achy-foot nurse, let's evaluate what might constitute an undue hardship:

- Has the employee's absence resulted in another employee not being able to take paid time off?
- Has the employee's absence resulted in decreased patient experience scores on the unit?
- Has the employee's absence resulted in increased overtime hours that exceed the budgeted allotted hours?
- Has the employee's absence resulted in the hiring or use of temporary or per diem employees that would have not normally been needed?

117

- How many other employees are on a leave of absence and what is their expected return-to-work date?
- What are some additional examples of the financial impact of the employee's continued absence?

What you cannot consider is whether the employee's continued absence would have an impact on the morale of the existing workforce (even if she continues to take selfies on the beach).

A case of undue hardship may be a little bit more difficult to prove for a nurse in a large healthcare setting than for a Director of Human Resources in the same organization. The case could be made that in a large healthcare organization, you may have hundreds of nurses that could fulfill the responsibilities of your nurse on leave while you may only have one Director of Human Resources.

Before embarking on the undue hardship analysis for a reasonable accommodation request, the first thing you should consider is the amount of additional time that the employee is requesting. If the amount of time is less than thirty days away, and you are considering terminating or backfilling the employee, the argument could easily be made that you would not have the opportunity to recruit and hire someone in less than thirty days.

Another common issue that keeps occurring in this scenario is when the employee continues to ask for an extension of their leave. Again, you must go through the same undue hardship analysis with each request. If you are not able to establish undue hardship for each request, you must grant the extension. There is no maximum amount of extended leave under the ADA, again unless undue hardship is demonstrated.

Returning to Work

After being on medical leave for almost 6 months, the beach-relaxing-foot-aching nurse is finally ready to return back to work. However, you are not quite so ready to have her back. You see while she was out, you hired a temporary employee to fill her void. The temporary employee has done a fantastic job in the four months that she's been with you. Her patients and colleagues really adore her (not to mention they really resent beach-relaxing-foot-aching employee for posting social media photos while she was away). You would like to keep temporary employee permanently and place beach-relaxing-foot-aching employee elsewhere. Can you?

As long as you return the employee to a nearly identical job, the answer is yes, but you must be very careful as "identical" to you may be perceived very differently by the employee. In nursing, working in a medical unit that has higher acuity than other units gives some nurses a sense of status and prestige in the organization. If you place them in a lower-acuity setting, this may be perceived as retaliation.

Another example would be if you have a teacher who was teaching advanced placement (AP) history when he went on leave, but when he returned he was told to teach a regular (non-AP) history class. The teacher may perceive the change as retaliation. Although the teacher will be working the same shift and in the same location and receive the same pay and benefits, they may feel like they've "lost" something because they were out on medical leave.

Many employers require a clearance to return to work, without restrictions, from the employee's medical provider before allowing them to return. That, too, is legal as long as this policy is consistently applied to everyone who is returning from leave. However, if the employee is not cleared for full duty and is asking to come back with restrictions, then the employer must again go through the same analysis as above and engage in the interactive process, determining if there is a reasonable accommodation and if not, embark on the undue burden analysis.

Intermittent Leaves

In our previous analysis, we discussed continuous FMLA leaves, that is, when an employee has taken their FMLA leave in consecutive days. However, employees are also entitled to take leave on an intermittent basis. Managing intermittent leaves can arguably provide the most headaches for organizations.

Some employees may be approved for an intermittent FMLA so they can attend scheduled appointments with their medical providers. For example, an employee may be returning to work from a knee surgery, but still needs to attend physical therapy a couple hours a day, a couple days a week. You know the days and times that that employee will be out of work and you are able to staff around his schedule accordingly. But what about the frequent lateness to work by the employee who has approved intermittent FMLA leave to care for a child with asthma?

All too often, managers are upset due to the unpredictably of intermittent FMLA leaves. An employee on an approved FMLA for their own serious medical condition, or that of their spouse, dependent, or parent, has the right under the FMLA to take time off work in increments (these increments can literally be in increments of minutes).

Managers often accuse employees of abusing incremental FMLA to avoid time and attendance issues at work. The story often goes that an employee is on discipline for excessive lateness and his next tardy will result in suspicion or termination. The same employee is also approved for intermittent FMLA to care for his child with asthma. "Coincidentally," now that the employee is facing disciplinary action for his tardiness, he now calls minutes before his scheduled shift to say that he will be late "because his son is wheezy and he needs to give him a breathing treatment."

If that doesn't sound familiar, try the case when a warehouse employee was approved for intermittent FMLA leave to care for his ailing father to include providing for his personal care and driving him to medical appointments. One day, he asked his supervisor to take a floating holiday the following day. His request was denied.

The employee responded by saying that he actually needed an FMLA day to take his father to an appointment. Because of his change of tune, human resources called his father's doctor's office to confirm whether there actually was an appointment scheduled. The doctor's office confirmed that there was no appointment.

The human resources department subsequently suspended the employee due to suspected FMLA abuse. After the suspension, the doctor's office called the human resources department and informed them that an appointment had just been made. HR attempted to confirm whether the employee had taken his father to the doctor on any of the days that he had taken FMLA leave, but the doctor's office refused to provide any additional information. The employee was ultimately terminated for FMLA abuse. The court sided with the company.[33]

To complicate matters more, an employee can have multiple, concurrent intermittent FMLA leaves. They can have separate intermittent leave for their own serious medical condition, their spouse, a child, and a parent all at the same time! I've seen it, and these were all legitimate, verified leaves. The good news is that the employee is still only given a total of 480 hours per 12 months for the leaves.

The courts in that case, and many others, have been vocal that employers can not only investigate suspected FMLA abuse, but can take prompt action as long as there is an honest belief that it is actual abuse. They have recognized that unfortunately, employees do in fact abuse both continuous and intermittent FMLA leave by moonlighting, using intermittent FMLA to take long weekends, partying and posting evidence on social media, going on holiday, golfing, shopping, to the beach, and or not caring for their loved ones as they say they are.

Practical Tips for Handling Misuse of FMLA

- Hire a third-party vendor to handle your FMLA leaves.
- Revise organizational policies on:
  - Moonlighting, and
  - Geographic and activity restrictions while on FMLA leave.

---

33 Scruggs v. Carrier Corp. 688 F.3d 821 (7th Cir. 2012).

- Ensure that the employee's medical certification is clear on the number of days and hours that the employee should be on leave.
- Consider hiring a private investigator for cases where you have an "honest belief" that there is abuse.

And there's more to it!

Here are some additional gray areas of FMLA that were not addressed during our scenario that is important for you to know.

1. When an employee initially asks for an FMLA leave, the employer must give the employee 15 calendar days to complete the medical certification.
2. An employer may, at its own expense, require that the employee obtain a second medical certification at the employer's choosing.
3. If an employee provides you with documentation that you deem to be incomplete or not sufficient, you may ask for additional information (in writing). This is particularly handy when it comes to intermittent leaves. You want the physician to be as specific as possible about the amount of time your employee needs away from work. If the employee does not provide the additional information in seven calendar days, you may deny the leave.

4.   If you require a Fitness for Duty certification upon an employee's return to work, the employee must be given sufficient notice.

5.   The Fitness for Duty certification should provide the health care provider with the employee's essential functions of the job and an FMLA designation.

6.   Although FMLA leave is unpaid, employees are still entitled to any bonus that they would have been entitled to if they had not gone on leave.

7.   Pregnant employees are entitled to FMLA prior to the birth of a child if they are experiencing a complication in their pregnancy due to a serious medical condition.

The Military & Leave

Service members deservingly receive additional leave protections. Regulated by the U.S. Department of Labor's Veterans' Employment and Training Service (VETS), the Uniformed Services Employment and Reemployment Act (USERRA) guarantees an employee returning from military service or training the right to be reemployed at his or her former job (or as nearly comparable a job as possible) with the same benefits. Unlike other federal statutes that have a minimum employee requirement, USERRA applies to virtually all employers regardless of size.

USERRA also impacts other laws that have been previously discussed in this book, adding an extra layer of protection for those who are covered under the act. Other impacted laws include: the Pregnancy Discrimination Act (PDA), the Family Medical Leave Act (FMLA), and the Americans with Disabil-

Let's get our veterans back to work!

According to the Bureau of Labor Statistics, veterans under the age of 24 have a higher unemployment rate than non-veterans of the same age.

Some of the challenges that young veterans face is coming back to a competitive job market, not being able to translate military skills to civilian work, and not being able to navigate through career progression in the work force as opposed to moving up the military ranks.

Many companies recognize the value of hiring a veteran and have implemented successful efforts to transition our veter-ans and military personnel into the private sector.

Companies such as Verizon have created tools that help military personnel to match their skills with the skills need-ed for open positions.

USAA gives job candidates who are military and their spouses priority when reviewing resumes.

AT&T has a military attraction team that specializes in recruiting veterans and helps to make their transition into a civilian career smooth.

If your organization is ignoring the capabilities that a veteran can bring to your workforce then you are simply missing out on great talent. YOU CAN'T DO THAT AT WORK!

ities Act (ADA). Other laws that we haven't discussed in this book, but also protect military employees, are state workers' compensation laws, state disability laws, and military leaves of absence.

The essence of most of these laws are that for employees who serve in the military, employers are required to hold their jobs and/or reemploy them upon their return. Examples of "serving" in the military means that an employee can be doing basic training, weekend work or training, active duty training, or actual active duty. The maximum cumulative military leave is five years. An employer must give employees who are covered under this act notice of their rights under USERRA and covered employees must give an employer proper notice of their intent to take leave (when feasible) and notice of intent to return to work, which triggers the employer to promptly re-employ the employee.

Covered employees maintain their seniority while on military leave and employers are prohibited from requiring them to take vacation or PTO time during this time. Additionally, when the employee returns from leave, they should not only be re-employed in the same or similar position, but also are entitled to the same pay they would have received had they had not left. For instance, if the employer had given all employees a 3% across-the-board increase every year while the employee was on leave, the employee's compensation should also reflect that increase for each year when he or she returns.

When a service member is informed that they will be deployed to a foreign country, that service member's spouse, parent, or child is entitled to qualifying exigency leave, which is an expansion of the FMLA for those serving in the armed forces. This leave gives qualifying employees the opportunity to handle life without the absent service member. The leave can be used to arrange child care, attend military ceremonies, or make arrangements necessary to prepare for the service member's departure. Eligibility for qualifying exigency leave is the same as eligibility for FMLA.

Unfortunately, many of our service members come back from active duty with disabilities. When this is the case, not only are they entitled to FMLA leave, but their family members are also entitled to military caregiver leave. Military caregiver leave gives up to 26 work weeks of unpaid leave in one 12-month period to care for the service member if she or he has a qualifying serious injury or illness. The serious injury or illness could be a result of their active duty or it could have been present before the service member's active duty, but was aggravated while they were active. It is important to add that if the service member returns to work with a disability, their disability should be analyzed just as it would for any other employee under the ADA as discussed in previous chapters.

Chapter 10

WELLNESS PROGRAMS AND GINA

Common mistakes that managers make:

---

67. Making employment decisions based upon an employee's genetic information
68. Developing wellness programs that are not compliant with the Genetic Information Nondiscrimination Act (GINA)

Wellness Programs and GINA

Common wellness programs offer incentives, discounts on health insurance, and additional perks to employees such as discounts on gym memberships, smoking cessation programs, and workplace weight loss programs. Employers tend to initiate these programs to facilitate a healthy workforce and to reduce healthcare costs, decrease absenteeism, and increase productivity and engagement. These programs commonly ask employees to participate in a biometric screening that measures body fat, blood pressure, cholesterol, or other indicators of potential disease. However, after the passage of GINA, some thought YOU CAN'T DO THAT AT WORK! Employers are essentially asking for or obtaining genetic information!

In May of 2016, the EEOC issued a final ruling on the use of collecting employees' and job applicants' genetic information as part of a bona fide wellness program.[34] Employers are permitted to collect genetic information as part of a wellness program that either incentivizes or penalizes employees as long as it is limited and "reasonably designed." For the program to be "reasonably designed," it:

- Must not be overly burdensome to employees; and must not be:
  - a subterfuge for violating Title II of GINA or other laws prohibiting employment discrimination; or
  - highly suspect in the method chosen to promote health or prevent disease.
- Participation incentives can be up to 30% of the total cost for self-only coverage.

Additionally, the program's purpose must not be to shift the cost of healthcare from the employer to the employee. The EEOC outlines several other considerations that must be made to avoid violating not only GINA, but also Title VII and HIPPA, the Affordable Care Act, ADA, DOL, HHS, and IRS regulations.

Health and Wellness at Work: Practical Considerations

Although I have outlined laws that protect an employee's job should they need time away from work or workplace flexibility

---

[34] U.S. Equal Employment Opportunities Commission. 2016. EEOC's Final Rule on Employer Wellness Programs and the Genetic Information Nondiscrimination Act. https://www.eeoc.gov/laws/regulations/qanda-gina-wellness-final-rule.cfm.

(a.k.a. reasonable accommodation) due to illness or disability, there are still many common scenarios that an employee may encounter in which they would not be covered by law. Remember Marissa Mayer who was hired as the CEO of Yahoo! while six months pregnant? Well, one of the reasons why she might have had to build that nursery in her office is because she was ineligible for FMLA (under federal law; California law may have offered her protections). Unlike ADA, which is triggered during the application process, as discussed, there is a waiting period to become eligible for FMLA (12 months to be precise). And remember, an employee's employer must have 50 or more employees to be eligible for that! Additionally, although you can be accommodated for your own disability under the ADA upon hire, disability accommodations do not apply to family members. Furthermore, the scope of the definition of "immediate family member" is small and only consists of an employee, their spouse, their dependents, and their parents. What happens when a grandparent becomes ill and you are their only family member close by? Or if it is an in-law, aunt or uncle, or as I have seen several times, your adult independent children? You simply have no federal job protections in those situations.

Many organizations recognize that while federal laws on this subject may seem broad and overreaching at face value, in reality they are not. I will discuss in the next chapters how under federal law, employees are not entitled to even one day off and can be worked as many hours as there are in a day as long as they are paid for those hours. Great places to work not only comply with leave and disability laws, but extend their workplace flexibility beyond their scope. Tech giants like Netflix offer 52 weeks of paid parental leave! That's unreal!

But if you're an employer, you're probably thinking, there's no way I can offer unlimited sick time! I would have to close my doors! Maybe you're right, but this is what you can do:

- Offer short-term disability (STD) supplemental benefits. STD is separate from FMLA. An employee can enroll in short-term disability benefits when they enroll in medical benefits upon hire and STD could provide income during their leave if they have yet to accrue PTO time.
- Offer paid parental leave like Netflix. Sure, you may not be able to offer 52 weeks, but time off to spend bonding with a newborn that wouldn't be required by law is a check in your favor as an employer.
- Offer personal leave-of-absence options. Personal leaves of absence give employees the ability to expand the scope of their leaves to care for grandparents, aunts and uncles, and in-laws.
- Offer sick bank sharing and employee assistance programs. Both of these options give colleagues the opportunity to help each other out in times of need, but also is not as impactful to your budget.
- Just be sympathetic and empathetic. I once worked with a manager who hated FMLA and everything that came with it. She huffed in disbelief every time an employee was approved for a leave. Unfortunately, a young child of hers was in a very unfortunate accident and she had to take several months off work. Not only was her job protected for the first few months, but our employer constantly assured her that there was no need to rush back to work and that

her job would be there safe and secure when she returned. You never know when you will be in the same shoes as your employees.

Considering these options has proven to be beneficial to employees in the long run. Not only will you be able to attract and retain top talent, but your organization will also be appreciated by your customers as they pay attention to how you treat your employees. Additionally, when employees can take time off for their health and be "stress-free," there can be a reduction in healthcare costs for employers. Job-protected leaves and disability laws were passed with the best of intentions. Remember, we all may need these protections one time in our career. If you know the laws and manage them lawfully, they can be a benefit rather than a liability or a burden.

PART III

WAGE AND HOUR

Chapter 11

FAIR LABOR STANDARDS ACT

Common mistakes that managers make:

69. Believing that federal law requires employers to provide employees sick days, holidays, vacations, and meal and rest breaks
70. Misclassifying non-exempt employees as exempt
71. Not compensating travel time when appropriate
72. Not compensating "on-call" time when appropriate
73. Avoiding overtime obligations by allowing employees to work off the clock
74. Providing access to work email at home to non-exempt employees without policy around it
75. Allowing non-exempt employees to work through lunch (but not compensating them for that time)
76. Not compensating employees for mandatory training and education
77. Making improper deductions from an exempt employee's salary
78. Treating independent contractors as employees

As much we may deny it and no matter how much passion we have for our jobs, what we are paid at work means a lot. Think about it. You read a job posting or receive a call from a recruiter about this intriguing new opportunity. It sounds like it's the job you've been waiting for all your life. At some point, whether raised by you or the recruiter, the topic of pay will come up. What is the starting salary for this position? What are your salary requirements? If the number isn't what you can live off of OR what you think you are worth, you will pass.

Today's job market is highly competitive. Although workers in the U.S. are increasing their expectations of non-traditional benefits and perks as discussed in the previous section, they are also demanding salaries that are aligned with the value that they bring to the organization. Workers are investing more in their careers. Because employees are no longer remaining with one employer for their entire career, they are continuing to develop and educate themselves for the next opportunity.

Recruiters are utilizing this platform to poach the top employees at organizations. I cannot count the number of messages I get on a weekly basis inviting me to throw my hat in the ring for an exciting job opportunity. I also cannot count the number of times, after getting those messages, that I have pondered whether or not my current role was providing me with the financial stability that I need to care for my family and whether or not I am being paid for my value.

Being paid for one's value is a growing concept that is continuing to evolve before our eyes. Last year, the state of Massachusetts passed a law banning employers from asking a job candidate about their salary history. The law also requires employers to tell job candidates, up front, what the compensation figure is based upon the job. This law was passed in an attempt to close the gender wage gap. While this law had some scratching their heads, I totally understand its intent and hope that many states and even Congress will follow suit.

Pay disparity between male and female workers is wide. Most of the disparity is due to the historical implications of having a predominantly male workforce. A person's salary history has been historically defined mostly by the years that they have in the workforce. The more experience you have, the more money you get. If a woman chooses to take time out of the workforce, she then loses work experiences and despite her qualifications, that and that alone could adversely impact her pay.

Moving forward, when she applies for a job and the potential employer asks her about her salary from her last job, which may have been three years ago, they use that salary information as a starting point for salary negotiations. Many women don't feel empowered or confident enough to argue their worth outside of their actual time at work and the potential success that they could bring to an organization. Thereby, females have ended up with lower salaries than their male colleagues. Because of this draconian way of determining compensation, there have been instances where female managers were paid less than their male direct reports that may have more time in the organization!

Scrapping the salary history question forces employers to:

- First, perform a comprehensive job evaluation, that is, determining: What is the relative worth of the role in the organization?
- Next, conduct a job analysis to find inconsistencies and inefficiencies: Which tasks should be done, and whom should they be done by?

- Then, re-examine job descriptions to really analyze the level of responsibilities and qualifications that the job applicant needs to be successful in the role.
- Finally, determine the appropriate pay structure.

Once an organization has completed those steps (which is easier said than done), then they have no need to ask for a salary history. They can simply inform the candidate of their pay range and negotiate within that. Done!

Before an organization can begin to determine whether or not their salaries are competitive enough to attract and retain top talent, they must first ensure that they are meeting the minimum requirements of federal wage and hour laws. This section will explain an employer's obligation under the Fair Labor Standards Act and the Equal Pay Act.

Fair Labor Standards Act

Everybody who's anybody in the workplace knows that for the past several months, organizations have been in absolute chaos in response to the new overtime regulations that were handed down by the Department of Labor, the regulatory agency that regulates:

- The Federal Minimum Wage
- Child Labor
- Recordkeeping
- Equal Pay
- And, yes, you guessed it, OVERTIME.

The new overtime rule would have made millions of employees across the US eligible to receive at least one-and-a-half times their regular rate of pay after 40 hours of work in a workweek. At the time of writing this book, the new rule has temporarily been blocked. The rules and regulations regarding overtime were already complex and posed significant challenges for employers. We will discuss those challenges and why the proposed overtime rule has employers screaming for mercy!

There are no federal laws that mandate employers in the United States to give employees sick days, vacation days, holidays, severances, meal or rest breaks, pay raises, or fringe benefits.

Basically, in the US, under federal law, an employee can work 24 hours a day, seven days a week, 52 weeks a year without a break – as long as you're paid for those hours accordingly (which is going to be quite expensive for your employer and a health and safety concern as well)!

However, depending on what you do for your organization, it may not even be that expensive. Meaning, some employees can work that same 24 hours a day, 7 days a week, 52 weeks a year and bring home the same paycheck week after week after week. Let's discuss how.

Employees who work for organizations that engage in interstate commerce, producing goods for interstate commerce, or handling, selling, or otherwise working on goods or materials that have been moved in or produced for such commerce by any person, are covered by the FLSA.

A covered enterprise is the related activities performed through unified operation or common control by any person or persons for a common business purpose and:

1. whose annual gross volume of sales made or business done is not less than $500,000 (exclusive of excise taxes at the retail level that are separately stated); or

2. is engaged in the operation of a hospital, an institution primarily engaged in the care of the sick, the aged, or the mentally ill who reside on the premises; a school for mentally or physically disabled or gifted children; a preschool, an elementary or secondary school, or an institution of higher education (whether operated for profit or not for profit); or

3. is an activity of a public agency.

Got it? Ok!

Employees who are employed in organizations as stated are classified as either exempt or non-exempt. All employees are eligible for overtime pay. Again, meaning if they work more than 40 hours in a work week they are to be paid one-and-one-half times their regular rate of pay for the time worked over 40 hours in a defined workweek. This means that they are not exempt from overtime (hence the meaning non-exempt).

What is Work?

Let's step back for a minute and talk about what qualifies as work since some organizations have challenges determining what compensable work time is for non-exempt employees.

Neither the Fair Labor Standards Act nor the Department of Labor has defined work for us exactly. They only address what the "workday" is in a very legalese way: "periods of time between the commencement of the employee's first principal activity and the completion of his last principal activity on any workday must be included in the computation of hours worked."

So, I guess it all boils down to this: What is a "principal activity?" There are a lot of common principal activities in a workday, and most of what you do at work is work, thus if you're a non-exempt employee, you will be paid to do it. However, there are several gray areas of not-so-principal activities that land organizations in the most trouble as the time is often considered immaterial and thus not compensable. But nothing could be further from the truth.

Here are some common examples of compensable time that employers believe are not compensable.

Commuting

- Traveling to and from work is not considered compensable time. However, let's say an organization asks an employee to stop on his way in to pick up some supplies needed for a project. That travel time would be compensable.
- Traveling from work site to work site as part of regular job duties would be paid time.
- Traveling "out of town" that keeps an employee from his home overnight is working time and should be compensated. However, if an employee is a passenger in an automobile, plane, train, bus, boat, etc. outside of normal working hours, then that may not be considered time worked.

An important consideration for commuting time is that in most cases, time and distance that is normally spent commuting from home to an employee's normal work site does not have to be compensated.

On-Call and Waiting Time

Determining whether or not on-call and/or waiting time is compensable can also be tricky for employers. There are many different ways that an employee can be considered to be on-call. However, it all boils down to the number of constraints that have been placed on the employee.

Let's examine:

ON-CALL COMPENSABLE	ON CALL NON-COMPENSABLE
Required to remain on work site (even though you may be eating, sleeping, or watching TV) with no freedom to leave is considered worked time.	If you are off-site and have freedom to engage in personal activities with little to no interruption, then the time spent "on-call" is usually not compensable.
If you can leave the work site, but must leave a number where you can be reached, stay in the near geographic region and are frequently called with little to no use of personal time while off-site would be compensable time.	

If an employee is at work, clocked in, and is just simply waiting around for work to do, then that waiting time is compensable.

Working Off the Clock Issues

Working off the clock usually is a result of either the employer or employee avoiding overtime pay. YOU CAN'T DO THAT AT WORK! The most frequent example of an employee avoiding overtime is when the employer has specifically directed employees to complete their work during the scheduled shifts and has prohibited the use of overtime to do so.

An employee who fails to complete their work during the shift is caught between a rock and hard place of either being disciplined for not completing their work or simply clocking out and continuing to work. They have made the decision to lose overtime pay rather than get in trouble for job performance.

An employer sometimes directs employees to work off the clock to avoid the financial implication, but still wants the work completed. YOU CAN'T DO THAT AT WORK! However, if an employer has knowledge, actual or constructive, of an employee working overtime hours (or any hours at all for that matter) they must be compensated.

Meal Periods

Meal periods can often land employers in a lot of trouble with not only the federal Department of Labor, but also with many state agencies that oversee wage and hour regulations in the workplace.

Although meal and rest breaks are not mandatory under federal law, many employers do give their non-exempt employees time to eat. This is usually because the employer knows that employees need a break to rest and rejuvenate so that they can be more productive during the second half of their day, or because it is mandated by state law.

Usually, meal breaks that are 20 minutes or shorter are compensated. However, anything over that time is often considered an unpaid meal break. If that is the case, then employees should not be engaging in any form of work and should be completely "on break." Many employees (especially those who have a desk job) often eat and work, although they have clocked out. They believe that because it is voluntary and they just want to "catch up on things" that this is ok. YOU CAN'T DO THAT AT WORK! Employees must be paid for all time worked even if it is not under the direction of the employer.

Working Lunches

Some employers mistakenly believe that if they provide lunch to employees while they are attending a meeting or training that they do not have to compensate for that time. They are sadly mistaken. This time is not being used for the employee's own personal time away from work and must be compensated.

Training and Education

Generally, four criteria must be met for training and education time to be non-compensable:

> Not during normal work hours
> Voluntary
> Not job related
> No other work is concurrently being performed.

If one or more of these criteria is not met, then the hours must be compensated.

Attached to Your Phone!

If all of your employees have access to their work email either by a webmail app or by syncing their email with their phone, you may be in trouble.

Non-exempt employees must be paid for all hours worked. Some non-exempt employees may be working compensable time if the amount of time that they are responding to emails is more than de minimis.

De minimis is "infrequent and insignificant periods of time beyond the scheduled working hours, which cannot as a prac-tical matter be precisely recorded for payroll purposes.

For example, if an employee simply answers, "yes" or "ok," that may be considered de minimis thus non-com-pensable.

However, if the employee is sending those short words constantly off the clock and/or are sending substantive email responses, that time may ex-tend beyond de minimis. Recommendations:

- Implement a working off the clock policy that discourages non-exempt employees from working from home.
- Minimize sending non-exempt emails during their non-working time as they may feel obligated to respond.
- If it is necessary to send a non-exempt employee an email during non-working hours, be clear that they shouldn't respond until working hours and be prepared to compensate if the work is more than de minimis.

Reporting Pay

Federal law does not require employers to pay reporting pay. Reporting pay means that an employee shows up to a job, but there is no work and the employer sends them home. Some states require four or so hours to be paid in this instance, but it is not required by federal law.

Again, all of the scenarios outlined above are only applicable if employees are considered non-exempt, meaning they are eligible to receive overtime pay.

But what makes an employee exempt from overtime? This is where it gets a tad... or well, a lot more complicated.

There are six exemptions from overtime.

Executive Exemption:

- The employee's primary duty must be managing the enterprise, or managing a customarily recognized department or subdivision of the enterprise;
- The employee must customarily and regularly direct the work of at least two or more other full-time employees or their equivalent; and
- The employee must have the authority to hire or fire other employees, or the employee's suggestions and recommendations as to the hiring, firing, advancement, promotion or any other change of status of other employees must be given particular weight.

Administrative Exemption:

- The employee's primary duty must be the performance of office or non-manual work directly related to the management or general business operations of the employer or the employer's customers; and
- The employee's primary duty includes the exercise of discretion and independent judgment with respect to matters of significance.

Professional Exemption:

- The employee's primary duty must be the performance of work requiring advanced knowledge, defined as work, which is predominantly intellectual in character and which includes work requiring the consistent exercise of discretion and judgment;
- The advanced knowledge must be in a field of science or learning; and
- The advanced knowledge must be customarily acquired by a prolonged course of specialized intellectual instruction.

Creative Professional Exemption:

- The employee's primary duty must be the performance of work requiring invention, imagination, originality, or talent in a recognized field of artistic or creative endeavor.

Computer Employee Exemption:

If compensated on an hourly basis, at a rate not less than $27.63 an hour:

- The employee must be employed as a computer systems analyst, computer programmer, software engineer, or other similarly skilled worker in the computer field performing the duties described below; and
- The employee's primary duty must consist of:
  a) The application of systems analysis techniques and procedures, including consulting with users, to determine hardware, software or system functional specifications;
  b) The design, development, documentation, analysis, creation, testing or modification of computer systems or programs, including prototypes, based on and related to user or system design specifications;
  c) The design, documentation, testing, creation or modification of computer programs related to machine operating systems; or
  d) A combination of the aforementioned duties, the performance of which requires the same level of skills.

Outside Sales Exemption:

To qualify for the outside sales employee exemption, all the following tests must be met:

- The employee's primary duty must be making sales (as defined in the FLSA), or obtaining orders or contracts for services or for the use of facilities for which a consideration will be paid by the client or customer; and
- The employee must be customarily and regularly engaged away from the employer's place or places of business.

Highly Compensated Employees

Highly compensated employees performing office or non-manual work and paid total annual compensation of $100,000 or more are exempt from the FLSA if they customarily and regularly perform at least one of the duties of an exempt executive, administrative or professional employee identified in the standard tests for exemption.

Additionally, to qualify for any exemption from overtime, an employee must also meet the salary basis requirement. The salary basis requirement states that an employee must not make less than $455 per week on a salary basis. Sales employees, teachers, and employees practicing law or medicine do not have to meet the salary basis requirement to be exempt from overtime.

Losing Exempt Status

Even if an employee meets the requirements for being exempt from overtime, they still run the risk of losing their exemption if an employer has an "actual practice" of making improper deductions from the employee's salary.

Employers can only make deductions from an exempt employee's pay in the following circumstances:

- If the exempt employee is absent from work for one or more full days for personal reasons other than sickness or disability.
- If the exempt employee is absent for one or more full days due to sickness or disability and the deduction is made in accordance with a bona fide plan, policy, or practice of providing compensation for salary lost due to illness.
- To offset amounts employees receive as jury or witness fees, or for military pay; for penalties imposed in good faith for infractions of safety rules of major significance for unpaid disciplinary suspensions of one or more full days imposed in good faith for workplace conduct rule infractions.
- For the full salary in the initial or final week of employment, or for weeks in which an exempt employee takes unpaid leave under the Family and Medical Leave Act.

It is important to highlight that although an employer may deduct PTO, vacation, and/or sick time for a full or partial day's absence, such a reduction may only be made providing that the employer has an established benefit plan. However, the reduction in the accrued PTO hours must not result in a reduction of the employee's guaranteed salary for the week. Although an employee may not have any vacation time, PTO, or sick time accrued, or have a negative balance, payment of the employee's salary must be made in the case of a partial-day absence for personal reasons of sickness or accident.

The exemption will not be lost if the deductions are considered to be isolated or inadvertent and if the employer reimburses the employee for the improper deductions. However, if an "actual practice" is determined, the exemption is lost during the time period of the deductions for employees in the same job classification working for the same managers responsible for the improper deductions.

Safe Harbor

If an employer (1) has a clearly communicated policy prohibiting improper deductions and including a complaint mechanism, (2) reimburses employees for any improper deductions, and (3) makes a good-faith commitment to comply in the future, the employer will not lose the exemption for any employees unless the employer willfully violates the policy by continuing the improper deductions after receiving employee complaints.

Misclassification Issues

Determining whether or not an employee can be exempt from overtime can be confusing and complex for some organizations, often resulting in lawsuits and penalties from the Department of Labor. This is especially true for those employees who do not fall within the highly compensated employee category, and whose jobs are not as clear cut under regulations like teachers, doctors, and lawyers.

Walmart had its share of misclassification issues as it was ordered to pay $4.8 million dollars in back pay, penalties, and fines when it misclassified its vision center managers and asset protection coordinators as exempt employees. The asset protection coordinators were responsible for store security and could not arguably fall into one of the five categories of exemptions. Although the vision center managers may have had the responsibility of supervising other employees, their primary duties were to sell contact lenses, glasses and frames, and other optical services to customers.

The Vision Center Manager title is an example of when employers cannot just call someone a manager, executive, professional, etc. and expect them to qualify for an exemption under the FLSA. The employee must actually perform the job functions or be qualified under the descriptions of each exemption.

Lowe's found this out the hard way when the retailer paid 9.5 million dollars to store-level human resources managers who claimed that they were misclassified as exempt employees and were denied overtime pay. In their complaint, the HR managers alleged that while their job description outlined functions that would have qualified them as exempt employees, they actually primarily spent a substantial amount of their time completing repetitive and routine tasks that were reflective of non-exempt job duties. YOU CAN'T DO THAT AT WORK and still be exempt!

The Proposed Overtime Rule

Now that you have the foundational knowledge of who is eligible for overtime and the implications of misclassifying employees as such, I will explain the impact of the proposed overtime rule and why it sent many organizations into such frenzy.

Since the Fair Labor Standards Act was passed in 1938, it has been updated seven times increasing the minimum salary level requirement. In 2004, the Department of Labor established the Highly Compensated Employee Exemption, which exempted employees making more than $100,000 from overtime.

In 2014, President Obama once again challenged the Department of Labor to re-evaluate which white-collar workers are protected by the FLSA overtime requirements. The DOL looked at a number of factors to include setting the standard salary level equal to the 40th percentile of earnings of full-time salaried workers in the lowest-wage census region (currently the south) and also to ensure that employers are not running into the same misclassification issues as Lowe's by classifying employees as exempt only by title but not by function.

What resulted from their analysis was raising the salary basis requirement from $455 per week to $913 per week (2015 with set increases every three years) and increasing the HCE to $134,000. These new thresholds would have impacted 12.5 million employees. Some employees welcomed the changes, some did not. Employers panicked.

The employees who jumped for joy over these changes did so because they had been working long hours without the benefit of overtime pay. Remember, under federal wage and hour law, if you are an exempt employee, you can work 24 hours a day, 7 days a week, 52 weeks a year and bring home the same amount of pay. Under this rule, newly qualified employees would now be paid time and a half for time worked over 40 hours in a workweek.

Some newly qualified employees were not so thrilled to be included in this group. Some (especially those who had worked their way up through organizations) saw this as a "demotion" in a sense. These employees have enjoyed flexibility in completing their work. Some may work six hours during the "normal" work day, then work another four at home later in the evening. Under their new classification, they may lose this privilege and flexibility as they would need to punch in and punch out at their work location and probably be prohibited by their employer from accruing overtime.

Employers were put in a sticky situation. First, they needed to conduct a complete analysis of their organization to determine the impact by identifying currently exempt jobs with salaries that fall below the proposed new salary threshold for exempt employees, using $913 per week, or $47,476 per year.

Next, they had to determine whether or not they should bump employees who were close to the new threshold to the new one (to remain in the exempt status) or to reclassify those employees as non-exempt. Those employers who chose the latter were faced with an additional challenge. As stated before, organizations could require those previously classified exempt employees to work as many hours as needed to complete their work, but now they would have to complete that same work in 40 hours or pay overtime.

Misclassification of Employees can DRIVE an employer insane!

Uber and Lyft, two companies where drivers can use their own vehicles to transport customers have recently come under scrutiny by many state Departments of Labor as they have clas-sified their drivers as independent contractors.

Both Uber and Lyft argue that because the drivers set their own hours and schedules they are independent contractors.

The drivers of both companies argue that be-cause they are controlled on how they interact with customers, can be fired with little to no notice, and can be deactivated if they do not accept enough pick-ups while on duty, they are in fact employees.

If the drivers are successful, they can then be entitled to minimum wage requirements, over-time, unemployment benefits, and workers compensation benefits among other things.

The decision had to be made whether to:

- hire additional non-exempt staff to assist with completing the work within the 40-hour time frame;
- pay the now non-exempt staff lower wages to compensate for potential overtime pay; or
- keep this group at their same pay, but pay overtime.

None of these options were appealing to employers.

Employers also had to determine whether or not their employees were subject to the highly compensated standard, but were below its new proposed pay level—that is, between $100,000 and $122,148 per year, jobs that satisfied the full duties test of one or more exemptions, as opposed to the previously more relaxed duties standardly applicable for highly compensated employees.

States and industries that had high average salaries were not as impacted as others. Many organizations in the northeast and California were not as impacted as organizations located in West Virginia, Arkansas, and South Carolina, which had the greatest share of salaried workers who would have directly benefitted from raising the threshold, according to an article published by the Economic Policy Institute.[35] Additionally, those in office and administrative support occupations would have benefitted the most.

Although the proposed overtime rule is temporarily halted, most organizations had already gone through this in-depth analysis, made critical decisions, and had communicated those decisions and changes to their employees in anticipation of the December 1, 2016 effective date. Now those same organizations have had to once again sit back down at the table and make additional tough decisions. Should they continue with their communicated changes (whatever they were) and live with whatever the consequences, both financial and non-financial, good or bad? Or should they go back to those same employees and tell them it was business as usual?

---

35   Eisenbrey, R. & Kimball, W. 2016. "The New Overtime Rule Will Benefit 12.5 Million Working People." Economic Policy Institute. http://www.epi.org/publication/who-benefits-from-new-overtime-threshold/.

Independent Contractors

Organizations use independent contractors (IC) for a variety of reasons, including avoiding IRS obligations, workers' compensation and unemployment insurance, paying benefits and other legal responsibilities that come with hiring actual employees for your organization. In addition to avoiding some regulatory and legal obligations, ICs, or leased, temporary, casual, or contract workers give organizations flexibility to use the workers as needed and to bring in the knowledge and skill sets that may not currently exist within the organization, but are not needed full time. However, hiring ICs does not come without legal challenges that organizations often find themselves battling.

If an organization exercises too much control over its independent contractors, an IC may inadvertently become its employee, thereby mitigating the reasons that they were hired as an independent contractor in the first place. KGB USA, a text message and internet information provider, learned this lesson the hard way when it misclassified its employees as ICs or Special Agents, as they called them.

The "Special Agents" were hired to respond to text message inquiries and worked from home. They were paid according to the number of text messages that they responded to rather than on an hourly basis. YOU CAN'T DO THAT AT WORK! KGB violated minimum wage, overtime, and recordkeeping requirements under the FLSA. The Department of Labor determined that Special Agents were in fact employees of KGB and reached a settlement for 1.3 million for the 14,500 employees.

Guidance for differentiating employees from independent contractors:

1. If the organization has the right to control the manner and means of accomplishing the result or outcome of the worker, then the worker is an employee of that organization.

2. An employee is paid for his/her time and bears no risk of wage loss if the employer's product is unprofitable. By contract, an independent contractor has the opportunity to profit from the project and be impacted by the risk of loss, depending on the worker's managerial skill.

3. An employee is not required to invest in the employer's business. An independent contractor makes some investment in tools, equipment, supplies, and facilities appropriate for his/her business.

4. An employee may receive training. An independent contractor has the skills necessary to perform the task without additional training.

5. An employee enjoys a continuing relationship with the employer. An independent contractor generally works on one project and moves on, accepting additional projects when and if available.

6. An employee provides services that are essential to the employer's business and incorporated into its products and services.

Additional tips for avoiding independent contractor misclassification claims:

- Independent contractor agreements should outline the specific and clear outcomes that are expected of the IC and should avoid mentioning bonuses, vacation time, and work hours.
- Independent contractors should provide the organization with an invoice outlining hours worked and deliverables on a set schedule, rather than the organization paying the IC the same amount on a set schedule.
- Organizations should not provide ICs with company email addresses or business cards and should not provide too much direction on completing their deliverables.

The bottom line is that an independent contractor is fully responsible for how, where, and when they work so long as they deliver the outcomes they were contracted for.

Interns: They Are Employees Too?

You get a call from your best friend asking if you have any work that his 17-year-old daughter, who is entering her senior year of high school, can do for you over the summer break. Your best friend tells you that there is no need to pay her, he just wants her to learn about the responsibilities of getting up early and going to work. Additionally, she is very interested in learning more about your industry. You tell him he has perfect timing because your receptionist is going out on an FMLA leave for the next three months and that would be perfect for his daughter. She's even excited too! Perfect! Well, maybe not.

Because your friend's daughter is performing work that is actually a part of the operations of the organization and the work that she is performing would have actually have been performed by an actual employee. Your friend's daughter is your employee and entitled to the minimum wage and overtime.

For organizations in the for-profit sector, the Department of Labor has provided a six-part test to determine if your "interns" are really interns or employees.

1. The internship, even though it includes actual operation of the facilities of the employer, is similar to training which would be given in an educational environment;

2. The internship experience is for the benefit of the intern;

3. The intern does not displace regular employees, but works under close supervision of existing staff;

4. The employer that provides the training derives no immediate advantage from the activities of the intern, and on occasion its operations may actually be impeded;

5. The intern is not necessarily entitled to a job at the conclusion of the internship; and

6. The employer and the intern understand that the intern is not entitled to wages for the time spent in the internship.

Because all of the criteria are not met in our case, your friend's daughter is not an intern. This training for your industry is not similar to an education environment. While she might learn a few things here or there, unless you're in the business of answering calls, this is not an education environment. Additionally, the intern displaces, or rather temporarily replaces a regular employee and there is no inference that she would be working under the close supervision of existing staff. Last, she is providing an advantage to the organization as she is filling a spot that would have had to have been filled by a paid employee while the incumbent was out on FMLA.

The media and entertainment industry have recently been subjected to settlements with unpaid interns who worked in production for companies such as NBCUniversal, Viacom, and Lionsgate. These highly publicized, high-profile settlements have brought renewed attention to the issues of unpaid interns in the private sector. Lesson learned here. Organizations should spare doing their friends and/or family favors by babysitting their kids for the summer. When asked about providing an unpaid internship to "help out" around the office, the reply should be YOU CAN'T DO THAT AT WORK.

Chapter 12

THE EQUAL PAY ACT

Common mistakes that managers make:

---

79. Having pay disparity between males and females doing the same work
80. Having subjective performance evaluation criteria that results in pay disparity
81. Not addressing pay parity soon enough to avoid resetting the clock for legal action each time the unfair pay is distributed
82. Having policies that prohibit employees from discussing their pay with one another
83. Not providing flexible work arrangements so that women do not feel compelled to choose between work and family
84. Believing equal pay is limited to gender disparity

The Equal Pay Act (EPA) prohibits men and women from getting paid unequal pay for the same work for the same employer. Despite this regulation, according to the Institute for Women's Policy Institute, female full-time workers made only 80 cents for every dollar earned by men in 2015, a gender wage gap of 20 percent.[36]

In financial year 2015, there were 973 equal wage complaints filed with the EEOC, which shows little increase in the number of complaints in the previous decade. Of those 973 cases, 64% of them were found to have no reasonable cause for action. What is driving both the low number of complaints filed as well as the low number of successful claims is the fact that claims of discrimination involving pay are hard to prove.

In order to defend an allegation of pay disparity, an employer must show that the disparity was a result of:

- A seniority system
- A merit system
- A pay system based on quantity or quality of output
- Any other factor other than sex

Citibank unsuccessfully tried to assert one or more of these defenses when a female employee who had been with the company for 11 years was promoted into a management position at a Citibank service center with no raise or no bonus. She knew that her male predecessor was compensated $129,567 in 2008. She was only compensated $75,329 at the time of her promotion in 2009. She requested a market analysis to be conducted after she was again denied a raise and/or bonus two years later. She was later terminated from the company without any severance.

---

36 Institute for Women's Policy Research. "Pay Equity and Discrimination." Retrieved from http://www.iwpr.org/initiatives/pay-equity-and-discrimination#sthash.ioErAyHh.dpuf.

Citibank argued that it determined its employee's compensation based on seniority, experience, and merit, but the court didn't buy it, citing Citi's subjective performance evaluation criteria. YOU CAN'T DO THAT AT WORK! Citi also argued that it couldn't afford to give the female employee a raise or bonus due to the poor economy. The court didn't buy that argument either as they had paid other employees huge bonuses during that same time period.

One of the reasons the Citibank female employee was successful in her equal pay claims was that she had knowledge of her male predecessor's higher pay, and was able to take that knowledge and file her claim with the EEOC within the Statute of Limitations. Many employees (not just women!) are not armed with such luck! However, there is some help for employees to arm themselves with the information they need to make a claim and beat the clock in doing so!

The first piece of legislation signed by President Barack Obama was the Lilly Ledbetter Act of 2009, which restarts the statute of limitations clock every time an employee receives an unequal paycheck, bonus, or anything that has monetary value. Prior to the Lilly Ledbetter Act, the clock started when the employer's original pay decision was made, which ultimately only gave employees 180 days from that point to file a claim with the EEOC. Because employees do not usually have access to other employees' pay data, they are often uninformed of pay disparity. This act is a common-sense approach to equal pay challenges in the workplace.

The major challenge, however, is in knowing whether or not an employee is being paid less than their other-gender counterparts. The Institute for Women's Policy Research conducted another survey[37] that revealed that about "half of all workers [surveyed] report[ed] that the discussion of wage and salary information is either discouraged or prohibited and/or could lead to punishment." Even if there is no policy in place prohibiting salary sharing, the other half of workers are apprehensive about sharing such information. The courts, however, are starting to view such policies of prohibiting discussing salary information with fellow employees as a violation of the National Labor Relations Act.

The National Labor Relations Act of 1935 allows employees to engage in protected concerted activity.

Protected concerted activity as defined by the act is when "two or more employees take action for their mutual aid or protection regarding terms and conditions of employment." Chipotle learned this lesson the hard way when the restaurant fired an employee after he revealed his hourly wage on social media. The employees filed a complaint with the National Labor Relations Board (NLRB) and the board determined that YOU CAN'T DO THAT AT WORK. They ordered Chipotle to reinstate the employee and pay him back wages. The board stated that the employee engaged in protected concerted activity that allows employees to talk about wages, hours, and terms and conditions of their employment. (Learn more about protected concerted activity in the chapter on the NLRA).

When determining parity, it is not titles that count, but rather the content of the jobs. Specifically, employers may not pay men and women wages that are not equal if they

---

37   Institute for Women's Policy Research. 2014. "Pay Secrecy and Wage Discrimination." https://iwpr.org/publications/pay-secrecy-and-wage-discrimination-2/.

perform jobs that require "substantially equal skill, effort and responsibility, and that are performed under similar working conditions within the same establishment. The EEOC offers some guidelines on differentiating skill, effort, and responsibility.[38]

- **Skill**

  Measured by factors such as the experience, ability, education, and training required to perform the job. The issue is what skills are required for the job, not what skills the individual employees may have. For example, two bookkeeping jobs could be considered equal under the EPA even if one of the job holders has a master's degree in physics, since that degree would not be required for the job.

- **Effort**

  The amount of physical or mental exertion needed to perform the job. For example, suppose that men and women work side by side on a line assembling machine parts. The person at the end of the line must also lift the assembled product as he or she completes the work and place it on a board. That job requires more effort than the other assembly line jobs if the extra effort of lifting the assembled product off the line is substantial and is a regular part of the job. As a result, it would not

---

38 U.S. Equal Employment Opportunities Commission. "Facts about Equal Pay and Compensation Discrimination." Retrieved from https://www.eeoc.gov/eeoc/publications/fs-epa.cfm.

be a violation to pay that person more, regardless of whether the job is held by a man or a woman.

- **Responsibility**
The degree of accountability required in performing the job. For example, a salesperson who is delegated the duty of determining whether to accept customers' personal checks has more responsibility than other salespeople. On the other hand, a minor difference in responsibility, such as turning out the lights at the end of the day, would not justify a pay differential.

- **Working Conditions**
This encompasses two factors: (1) physical surroundings like temperature, fumes, and ventilation; and (2) hazards.

- **Establishment**
The prohibition against compensation discrimination under the EPA applies only to jobs within an establishment. An establishment is a distinct physical place of business rather than an entire business or enterprise consisting of several places of business. In some circumstances, physically separate places of business may be treated as one establishment.
For example, if a central administrative unit hires employees, sets their compensation, and assigns them to separate work locations, the

separate work sites can be considered part of one establishment.

According to a 2015 Council of Economic Advisers Brief, "experimental research" using "resume studies" show that "where only the name differs, gender affects whether the candidate is hired, the starting salary offered, and the employer's overall assessment of the candidate's quality." The study also acknowledges the increased complaints filed with the EEOC regarding gender discrimination.[39] Outside of compulsory federal laws, employers can and should take action to remedy the wage disparity within their organizations.

- Eliminate policies that prohibit employees from discussing their compensation. If an organization's pay practices are fair and non-discriminatory, there should not be an issue with transparency.
- Provide flexible working schedules so that employees are able to balance work obligations with family responsibilities. Studies have shown that when employees work from home they are actually more productive as they tend to want to "prove" that working from home actually "works"!
- Conduct an organizational pay gap analysis to determine if your pay practices are consistent across genders. Remember, you cannot reduce an

39 Council of Economic Advisers. 2015. "Gender Pay Gap: Recent Trends and Explanations." April Issue Brief. https://obamawhitehouse.archives. gov/sites/default/files/docs/equal_pay_issue_brief_final.pdf.

employee's pay to address pay disparity, but you can definitely increase the lower earner's salary.

Compliance with federal wage and hour laws is a BIG DEAL! 90% of all employment-related class-action suits are related to federal wage and hour violations and the number of overall wage and hour cases filed with federal courts has increased by 450% since 2000. The top settlements in 2015 equated to 2.5 billion dollars. The Wage and Hour Division of the Department of Labor is aggressive with investigating organizations' payroll and time and attendance records. In 2010, they launched several initiatives that helped them to raise awareness about wage and hour laws, including creating an app for employees that allows them to track their time at work to determine if they've been appropriately paid.

Usually, wage and hour violations are not a simple mistake by one manager regarding one employee, which is usually the case in employment discrimination suits. Rather, the organization usually has a systemic culture of not knowing what is compensable time, whether employees might have been misclassified as independent contractors, and how to determine if an employee is overtime eligible. In fact, many class actions can be so large that the actual payout per employee can be quite small compared to the amount of the settlement. For instance, the Brinker Restaurant Company settled with class-action plaintiffs for California meal and rest break violations for $56 million dollars! However, because the class so was large, the actual settlement amount per plaintiff was a measly $523 on average. The lesson learned from this case and many others is that although an employee may skip a meal, even of their own accord, they must still be compensated for that time worked.

Many states have wage and hour laws that are much narrower than federal law. For instance, federal law does not require employers to give employees a meal or rest break, but many states do. States such as New York and California go as far as to say when the meal or rest break must be taken. As such, it is important that organizations be in compliance not just with federal pay laws, but state laws as well. Additionally, employers should ensure that managers are well aware of your policies and take a "zero tolerance" stance of employees working without being compensated. Employers should additionally conduct audits of their practices to catch and remedy any federal and state violations to mitigate legal liability.

PART IV

THE NATIONAL LABOR RELATIONS ACT

Chapter 13

PROTECTED CONCERTED ACTIVITY

Common mistakes that managers make:

85. Not knowing the National Labor Relations Act (NLRA) protects all employees in the workplace, not just those in a union
86. Not understanding the connection between social media and protected concerted activity
87. Having zero-tolerance harassment policies that could potentially violate the NLRA
88. Having policies that require civility and respect
89. Thinking that because an employee has engaged in protected concerted activity that they are exempt from any adverse employment action

Only 3 out of 10 employees are engaged in the American workplace. Three out of 10! As discussed in Chapter 1, disengaged employees tend to be unproductive, have a high level of absenteeism, take more FMLA leaves, have more workers' compensation claims, and yes, you guessed it, sue! Some employees choose not to take any of these actions and take a different route after all other efforts have failed.

Membership in labor organizations have steadily declined in recent years. This is due to many reasons:
- The number of federal and states laws that prevent unfair treatment in the workplace.
- Competitive wages and benefits in industries that are predominantly unionized.
- Employees are now aware that unions are revenue genera-tor organizations who make their profits based on member-ship dues.
- Employers taking proactive measures to mitigate union organizing such as: educating their management teams on signs of union organizing and conducting surveys to measure employee satisfaction.

Let's think about some of the cases and scenarios that we've discussed so far in this book.

Hi! I'm Mary.

My boss is a jerk who disrespects me and my peers. Although we've complained to HR, nothing has been done because he's been able to operationally exceed organizational goals and is part of the good ole boy's circle. It is obvious that despite the high turnover in his area, he's not going anywhere. Additionally, I am always having to work overtime hours and am completely overwhelmed at work because so many other employees are on a leave of absence due to stress. It seems as if the only way you can get promoted around here is if you are a male. I can barely pay my bills and my friends who do the same job for other organizations make much more than me. I feel so under-appreciated and undervalued. Last month, the employees in my department heard that the company may be outsourcing our jobs to independent contractors. After I heard this rumor, I began to look for another job, but have been unsuccessful.

There are thousands, if not millions of Americans in the workplace who have the same sentiments as Mary. Employees mistreated in the workplace are being subjected to bullying by their supervisors, have few advancement opportunities, are underpaid, or fear losing their jobs, and have no support or concern from HR and/or organizational leadership, who know full well that while their work conditions are unacceptable, they are lawful. So that leaves them with one option: to elect a labor union to act on their behalf to negotiate better terms and conditions of employment. The National Labor Relations Act (NLRA) of 1935 allows employees to do just that.

The National Labor Relations Act provides all employees, even those who are not in a union or have no intent to join a union, protections in the workplace. This section will explore the protections afforded to employees, as well as what is considered unlawful conduct under the National Relations Labor Act.

The National Labor Relations Act = The Beginning of YOU CAN'T DO THAT AT WORK!

Prior to the 20th century, there were no federal protections for employees in the workplace. What that meant was that organizations were able to discriminate and harass employees just because of the way they looked, the color of their skin, their age, or their gender. Additionally, employers were not required to provide health insurance benefits, days off, the minimum wage, or a safe work environment. Although eventually employees began to form labor unions to advocate for better working conditions and organize strikes and protest if their demands weren't met, federal law did not protect this conduct and workers could be fired for engaging in it.

There was no such thing as employee engagement, talent management, or performance management. Diversity initiatives and affirmative action planning were foreign concepts. Consumers paid no attention to the social responsibility of an organization. In fact, both organizations and consumers were concerned with one thing and one thing only: supply and demand. The American consumer demanded goods and services and American companies supplied them at any cost.

An American worker would go to work not knowing if that day would be their last day, either because they would be fired due to the economy, or because their boss just didn't like them, or most horrifically, because they were severely injured on the job. There was no such thing as job security or satisfaction or work-life balance. The rich were getting richer, but despite the long, hard dreadful days at work away from family, the poor were getting poorer.

As America entered the 20th century, it became obvious that more and more Americans were transitioning from working on family farms or family-owned businesses to work on the front lines of America's growing industries. Thus more regulation was needed, beginning with The National Labor Relations Act of 1935 that gave workers the ability to form, join, and organize unions that could strike and protest harsh working conditions. These activities that employees could engage in are called protected concerted activity, and over the years what has been considered protected activity has expanded dramatically due to the increasing use of technology.

In Chapter 12, we discussed how the Chipotle employee was able to reveal his hourly rate on social media under the protections of the NLRA. Social media has certainly caused disruption in the way that organizations can manage conduct outside of the workplace and the liberties that are given to employees to reveal their work conditions to the world through social media is causing chaos.

What many organizations and managers have failed to understand is that NLRA not only regulates and protects who can form a union, how a union can be formed, and what kinds of employees can be in a union, but also it also protects employees who have absolutely no desire to form and/or join a union!

Protected concerted activity used to take the form of employees gathering in break rooms, parking lots, at each other's houses, etc. to discuss their terms and conditions of employment. At some point, employers got the message that this type of chatter was lawful and could not be disrupted and they could not retaliate against their employees for engaging in it.

Then between 2011 and 2012, the NLRB began to see an uptick of charges in organizational policies regarding social media that were unlawful and violated the NLRA's protections of employees' ability to engage in concerted activity. One of the first decisions in which the NLRB determined that an employer had engaged in unlawful conduct due to a social media posting involved five employees of a non-profit organization who posted Facebook postings about a coworker who intended to complain to management about their work performance. Specifically, one employee posted, "Lydia Cruz, a coworker, feels that we don't help our clients enough at [Respondent]. I about had it! My fellow coworkers how do u feel?" Four other employees responded to the post, objecting to the criticism by the employee. The employee at whom the criticism was aimed complained to her organization and the organization subsequently fired the original poster and the four responding posters, stating that the post constituted "bullying and harassment" of their coworker which violated their "zero tolerance" of such conduct. YOU CAN'T DO THAT AT WORK! The board considered the behavior not to be harassment, but rather just five employees discussing their terms and conditions of employment.[40]

Like the employer in this case, many organizations have policies that attempt to address potential social media posting issues. The employer in this case cited that the behavior of the employees violated their zero-tolerance harassment policy,

---

[40]   Hispanics United of Buffalo, Inc., 359 NLRB No. 37 (2012).

but the board has stated that some policies address both harassment and social media may be too broad and potentially violate the NLRA.

Employers may also violate employees' rights to engage in protected concerted activity if they require them to be happy, civil, or respectful at work. This was the case when the NLRB told one employer that its policy of "maintain a positive work environment by communicating in a manner that is conducive to effective working relationships with internal and external customers, clients, co-workers, and management" violated the NLRA! YOU CAN'T DO THAT AT WORK!

The following table looks at some examples of policy language that the board has found to have restricted an employee's right to engage in concerted protected activity.[41]

POLICY STATEMENT	WHY YOU CAN'T DO THAT AT WORK
Non-Disparagement Rule: making disparaging comments about the company through any media, including online blogs, other electronic media, or through the media.	Could be construed to restrict Section 7 activity, such as statements that the employer is, for example, not treating employees fairly or paying them sufficiently. Further, the rule contained no limiting language that would clarify for employees that the rule does not restrict Section 7 rights.

---

[41] National Labor and Relations Board. "The NLRB and Social Media." Retrieved from https://www.nlrb.gov/news-outreach/fact-sheets/nlrb-and-social-media.

Employees should avoid identifying themselves as employees of the company on external social media site "unless there was a legitimate business need to do so or when discussing terms and conditions of employment in an appropriate manner."	The policy "implicitly prohibit[ed] "inappropriate" discussions of terms and conditions of employment" and did not define what "appropriate" or "inappropriate" discussion of terms and conditions of employment would be.
A "savings clause" [that] provided that the policy would not be interpreted or applied so as to interfere with employee rights to self-organize, form, join, or assist labor organizations, to bargain collectively through representatives of their choosing, or to engage in other concerted activities for the purpose of collective bargaining or other mutual aid or protection, or to refrain from engaging in such activities.	Does not outline what discussions would be deemed to be appropriate.
A social media policy that prohibited employees from using social media to "engage in unprofessional communication that could negatively impact the employer's reputation or interfere with the employer's mission or unprofessional/inappropriate communication regarding members of the employer's community."	The rule contained examples of "clearly unprotected conduct, such as displaying sexually oriented material or revealing trade secrets; it also contained examples that would reasonably be read to include protected conduct, such as inappropriately sharing confidential information related to the employer's business, including personnel actions."

The social media policy "prohibited discriminatory, defamatory, or harassing web entries about specific employees, work environment, or work-related issues on social media sites."	The policy was replaced with one that "prohibited the use of social media to post or display comments about coworkers or supervisors or the employer that are vulgar, obscene, threatening, intimidating, harassing, or a violation of the employer's workplace policies against discrimination, harassment, or hostility on account of age, race, religion, sex, ethnicity, nationality, disability, or other protected class, status, or characteristic" that was found to be reasonable and not a violation of Section 7 rights.

What Is Not Protected Concerted Activity?

Individual Gripes

When an employee posted a comment to her Facebook after being reprimanded by her employer that included an expletive and the store name, four of her co-workers "liked" the status but did not comment. Her termination was held to be an individual gripe and not protected concerted activity. When she posted the comment, according to the board she "had no particular audience in mind. Additionally, she never suggested that she wanted to initiate any kind of 'group action.'" And, finally, she did not seek to "induce or prepare for group action or to solicit group support for her individual complaint."

Revealing Confidential and/or Proprietary Information about the Company, Other Employees, Customers, Patients, Etc.
A fire department lieutenant was terminated when he posted a picture of his computer screen that contained confidential information, including a caller's name, address, and phone number on Facebook. However, distinguishing between confidential information and personal information as the latter may be considered protected.

Where's the Balance?

With all the restrictions on what policies organizations are able to implement to ensure a positive and engaging workplace, many employers wonder how they can avoid running afoul of the NLRA, while also providing a harassment-free workplace as required by the EEOC and tort laws that I have previously explained in this book. The answer is not simple and should be analyzed on a case-by-case basis. For example, if an employee is demonstrating uncivil conduct to another employee and it has nothing to do with their terms and conditions of employment, then it is possible that you can lawfully address that employee's conduct. However, if an employee is caught being rude to a customer and in the course of the conversation the employee says, "I hate working here, it's a bad place to work," then the employer may run into some roadblocks with holding that employee accountable for their words and actions.

But remember, if an organization has a culture of a civil and respectful conduct that begins and is reflected by the behavior of its leaders, then most likely employees will act with civility and respect as well. This will mitigate an organization's need to create policies on this topic. I've said it before and I'll say it again: Employees can't be what they don't see.

Chapter 14

FORMING A UNION

Common mistakes that managers make:

90. Not responding to employees' concerns, resulting in them organizing a union
91. Not recognizing when union organizers (or SALTS) are active in their organization
92. Violating "TIPS" during the union campaign process that result in an unfair labor practice charge

In the previous chapter, you learned how employees can engage in protected concerted activity even when their intent is not to form a union. Now, we will explore protected concerted activity as it relates to employees forming and/or joining a union. Earlier in this section, you met Mary, who is unhappy at work because of a bad manager, unwanted overtime, job insecurity, and a lack of response to her concerns from human resources. When employees such as Mary begin to feel this way, they often believe they have no other option than to have someone else speak on their behalf with the hopes of improving their working conditions. This is usually achieved by electing a labor union to represent them in the workplace and to negotiate better terms and conditions of employment.

The Process

A labor union often seeks out organizations that have disengaged and unhappy employees such as Mary. They can get this intelligence in many ways, such as social media posts (that we described earlier in this section), websites that allow employees to leave comments about their organization, and by placing "salts." Salts are union organizers who apply for jobs within a targeted organization then begin the union organizing process by soliciting employees to sign a petition for the union to represent them.

Unions cannot organize an entire organization, but rather must identify what's called a bargaining unit. A bargaining unit is a group of employees with a community of interest. For example, a union cannot come into retail to establish and organize cashiers and stockroom workers under the same bargaining unit. They would have to choose one or the other. Once the bargaining unit has been identified, the union would then attempt to convince the members of that bargaining unit to sign a petition or authorization cards that will show support of forming the union. The union must get 30% of members of the identified bargaining unit to sign the authorization cards or petition in order to request an election to be held. If the union receives over 50% of signatures from the bargaining unit, then that is considered a card check election and the union is the official representative of those employees.

Once the union has demonstrated to the National Labor Relations Board (NLRB) that it has the 30% of the requisite signatures for an election to be held, the NLRB then notifies the organization, which can challenge the validity of the process, the signatures, or the bargaining unit. Once any challenges have been resolved, then the NLRB will schedule an election.

Prior to the election date, the union and the organization embark on a campaign just like you would see prior to any election. The union will make its case for why employees should join the union and the organization will make its case for why employees should not join the union.

During the campaign process, managers will focus their efforts on communicating the following:

- That the union is a for-profit organization that you have to pay dues to join. They may even be able to make the case that you may come out with less in your check than you did before unionizing because you are now paying dues.
- Explaining that typically, employees who are not in the union are not rewarded for their performance, but salary increases are usually based on a set schedule outlined by the collective bargaining agreement.
- Comparing benefits, pensions, etc. to determine how employees will benefit financially from not being a union.
- Outlining all the wonderful non-traditional benefits that the organization provides to its employees, such as tuition assistance, rewards and recognition events, and other development programs.
- That employees will lose the availability to go to court to settle employment disputes as they now

will be settled with an arbitrator and remedies are very limited.

During the campaign, the union will focus their efforts on communicating the following:

- That employees have tried to improve their terms and conditions of employment by seeking assistance from organizational leadership and HR, but have been unsuccessful.
- That they can negotiate better wages, benefits, and pension packages.
- That employees can no longer be terminated without cause as the terms and conditions of employment are now outlined by the collective bargaining agreement.
- How seniority matters will be handled when it comes to transfers, promotions, and layoffs under a collective bargaining agreement.
- That employees will always have an advocate when in dispute with the organization.

There are certain parameters as to what an organization can and cannot do during the campaign process. Employers are not allowed to:

- Make **Threats!** An employer cannot threaten to close the organization if it is unionized or threaten to terminate an employee for voting for the union.
- **Intimidate** employees. Intimidation can be construed as using the power of the employer to coerce an

employee not to join a union. Intimidation falls just a little short of making a threat.
- Make **promises** to the employees. At this point, an employer cannot say, "If you do not vote for a union, we promise to give salary increases.
- **SPY.** Employers cannot spy on union organizing efforts such as sending a non-member of the bargaining unit to where they know the union is meeting with potential bargaining unit members.

Violations of these types are called unfair labor practices. If it is determined that an organization has engaged in an unfair labor practice, the NLRB will ask them to desist the behavior and to make any employee who was affected by the behavior whole (reinstatement, payment of back pay, etc.).

Quickie Elections

Just a couple of years ago, the period to campaign for votes took on average about 42 days before the election. This gave both the union and the organization time to adequately make their arguments so that employees were well informed when making their decisions. However, at the beginning of 2015, the NLRB passed the "quickie election" rule that significantly decreased the amount of time that an organization and an employer had to campaign. Now, the average campaign period is about 23 days (however there are some reports of a less than 14-day campaign period). This has resulted in more elections being won in favor of the union. You're probably wondering why this is the case?

Remember, for a union to get an election, they must collect 30% of signatures or authorization cards from members of the bargaining unit. That 30% is more than likely definite "yes" votes for the union (unless the employees didn't know what they were signing, as can be the case sometimes). Now both the union and the organization need the remaining 70% of the bargaining unit to vote in their favor. Among that 70%, some are definitely a "no" to the union, so it is the undecided that the campaign is geared toward.

The undecided are a special bunch. Along with hearing campaign speeches from both the union and their organization, they are being persuaded by their peers and colleagues. Many will say to keep the peace, "I just won't vote at all." That stance is problematic... for the organization. A no vote is a vote for the union. Why? To win the election, the union must receive 50% plus 1 of votes of the entire number of people in the bargaining unit regardless of whether or not they voted. The smaller the bargaining unit, the easier that is to accomplish. Let's look at an example.

- The bargaining unit has 30 employees.
- 30% of the employees signed a petition, so we're going to assume that 9 employees are a definite yes.
- The union needs 16 employees to vote yes to win the election. They already have 9 votes, so they need only 7 more votes. If 3 employees decide not to vote, the union then only needs 4 more employees to vote yes (other than the original 9 who signed the petition).

It is as simple as that!

The election takes place by secret ballot on the employer's premises. A representative from the NLRB, the employer, and the union are all present for the election. The election environment must be reflective of "laboratory conditions," meaning that the conditions in which the elections take place should be as ideal as possible so employees can be free of inhibitions to voting in the way that they choose.

There are many other twists and turns of the NLRA that are not explored in this book. In fact, be on the lookout for a subsequent book entitled *You Can't Do That at Work: Labor Relations Edition.* In the meantime, please consider the practical considerations outlined below.

Practical Considerations

The NLRA's reach is far and wide and protects much more than union organizing activity. What is protected concerted activity continues to expand and evolve. In addition to social media, websites such as glassdoor.com and indeed.com allow employees to leave comments about their current or former employer.

To avoid employees airing your "dirty laundry" for the world to see and to "unfair labor charges" with the NRLB, here are some recommendations:

- Train all managers on protected concerted activity under the NLRA. The training should include what is protected and what is not and how to respond in either scenario.

- The human resources department should be a credible, reliable place of trust that employees can go to share their concerns. Remember, when employees believe they are not being heard by HR or organizational leadership, they will take any and all avenues to be heard. Even if that means social media.
- Be proactive by measuring the level of engagement in your organization. This can be accomplished by conducting an employee engagement survey, focus groups, pulse surveys, and analyzing other data that measure engagement. If it is determined that your workforce, or parts of it, is disengaged, take immediate action. If employees see you care, they are less likely to take their concerns outside of the organization.
- If employees in your organization embark on an organizing campaign, take the advice from this book to avoid charges of unfair labor practices.

PART V

UNLAWFUL RETALIATION

Chapter 15

RETALIATION – THE FINAL FORM OF DISCRIMINATION

Common mistakes that managers make:

---

93. Inadvertently engaging in retaliatory conduct after an employee has engaged in protected activity
94. Retaliating against former employees
95. Not knowing that even long periods of time between protected activity and an adverse action can result in retaliation
96. Not knowing that retaliation claims are the most filed with the EEOC

Throughout this book, we have discussed several laws that tell employees, employers, and job candidates what YOU CAN'T DO AT WORK! After reading this book, an employee may realize that they have been unlawfully harassed or discriminated against, have not been compensated for time worked, or that their employer has interfered with their leave and/or disability rights. An employee can and should report the unlawful activity to their organization's human resources team and/or the appropriate regulatory agency. If after they report the unlawful conduct, they are subjected to (1) tangible negative actions by their employer such as job loss, demotion, an undeservingly poor job evaluation or (2) non-tangible antisocial actions such as harassment, hostility and intimidation, they have been subjected to yet another form of discrimination called *unlawful retaliation.*

Retaliation can be a scary topic for employers. An employee need not prove that the original underlying discrimination actually occurred, only that they were retaliated against because they reported the unlawful conduct.

Because of the broad spectrum of what can be considered retaliation, employers often find themselves in three places along a spectrum.

On one end, an employer may think that because the employee has engaged in the protected activity of reporting alleged unlawful conduct, that the employee is exempt from discipline, from discussion regarding poor performance, and/or termination. Nothing can be further from the truth.

In the middle, some employers "unknowingly" engage in retaliatory conduct after an employee has engaged in protected activity.

Finally and unfortunately, on the other end of the spectrum there are instances where employers do outright retaliate against employees who report alleged unlawful behavior.

This chapter will explore each of these three scenarios as it relates to unlawful conduct under the oversight of the EEOC and the Fair Labor Standards Act.

The False Accuser at Work

Every organization has an employee who constantly lodges complaints of discrimination and/or harassment by their supervisor and/or peers. A diligent employer investigates all allegations of unlawful conduct.

However, it can be frustrating and time-consuming to investigate constant, meritless, frivolous complaints from the same employee.

What can an employer do to address false accusations of harassment in the workplace without being on the hook for a retaliation claim?

One company found out when it fired a constant complainer during a reduction in force. The employee had lodged many complaints against his supervisor that were found to be merit-less. The company concluded that he was "sensitive to feed-back" and should "move on."

The court concluded YOU CAN DO THAT AT WORK! The company's response to the allegations and the employee's termination were appropriate.

The company was able to demonstrate that the employee was a disruptive, poor-performing employee who was downsized. The conduct was not retaliatory for his previous complaints.

Case closed!

Under the EEOC, a retaliation claim challenging action taken because of EEO-related activity has three elements:

1. **protected activity**: "participation" in an EEO process or "opposition" to discrimination;
2. **materially adverse action** taken by the employer; and
3. a requisite level of **causal connection** between the protected activity and the materially adverse action.

Both current and former employees can raise an allegation of retaliation, even when the unlawful conduct opposed is not committed by the same employer who retaliated. An example here would be that an employee leaves Company A and is hired by Company B.

Subsequent to being hired by Company B, he files a complaint with the EEOC alleging that Company A violated Title VII. Company B finds out about the suit and terminates the employee during his probationary period, citing "he wasn't a good fit."

The employee later learns that Company B sees him as a potential troublemaker because of his pending claim with the EEOC. YOU CAN'T DO THAT AT WORK! The termination by Company B could be viewed as retaliation, although the alleged discriminatory practice did not occur at Company B. The same has held to be true when it is revealed during the reference checking process that an employee was engaged in prior legal action with a company.

Protected Activity

In the chapter on the National Labor Relations Act, we discussed when two or more employees engage to improve their terms and conditions of employment that is considered protected concerted activity. However, when only one employee acts to protect themselves from unlawful activity at work, that is considered protected activity sans the concerted. But what activity exactly is protected? This is the first element of proving a retaliation claim as described previously. Let's look how the EEOC describes protected activity.

Protected activity is that which is protected by the law to include "participating" in an EEO process or "opposing" discrimination. It is important to take a moment and differentiate between "participating" and "opposing."

When a person is involved in any manner in a EEOC proceeding, they would have "participated." This can include protecting, testifying, assisting, or preparing an affidavit in conjunction with a proceeding or investigation under any law regulated by the EEOC, even if the allegations are invalid or unreasonable.

A couple of examples of the extension of the "participation" clause of retaliation include an employee who had volunteered to participate in a proceeding corroborating a plaintiff's allegation of sexual harassment, but who was never called. Although she was never called to testify, her willingness to participate was protected under the "participation" clause. The court said in that case that employees who participate "in any manner" are protected from retaliation.[42]

---

[42]   Jute v. Hamilton Sundstrand Corp., 420 F.3d 166, 175 (2d Cir. 2005).

A more interesting case that provides an interesting twist to the "participation" clause was when a female receptionist at a paper company filed a sexual harassment suit against her employer due to an accepted atmosphere of sexually explicit jokes, comments, cartoons, and profanity that were frequently circulated around her office and that continued despite her complaints. During depositions for her sexual harassment suit, male employees reluctantly participated, and a male employee testified that he had participated in some of the offensive conduct.

The company eventually settled with the plaintiff, but subsequently terminated the male employee who had admitted to being involved in the acts of sexual harassment during depositions. YOU CAN'T DO THAT AT WORK! The court found the actions by the employer to be retaliation, as his termination was not a result of the harassing conduct itself, but because he "participated" in a Title VII suit by testifying.

Now, let's explore the opposition clause which protects a broader range of conduct than the participation clause.

If an employee believes that his or her employer has engaged in a form of employment discrimination and opposes it, that opposition is considered protected activity. The form in which the employee communicates his opposition can come in many ways and does not have to be explicit, as in the example that the EEOC gives of an employee accompanying another employee to HR to file a complaint of discrimination. Or, it was protected activity when an employee complained about other employees being harassed in the workplace although they were not a member of the group being harassed.[43]

---

[43]   Ray v. Henderson, 217 F.3d 1234, 1240 (9th Cir. 2000).

An employee's opposition to discriminatory conduct does not have to be communicated to the employer itself to be protected. There have been many cases where an employee has opposed discriminatory behavior by communicating their opposition to the police, attorneys, fellow employees, or not even by their own initiative, but as part of an employer's own investigation as was the case when a supervisor refused to fire a subordinate because the firing would be found to be unlawfully discriminatory.

Again, however, employers need not be scared to discipline, terminate, or engage in performance discussions with employees in fear that they may scream retaliation. One employee learned that lesson the hard way when she used the opportunity during an internal sex discrimination investigation to make "superficial" comments about her boss and "harp[ed] on issues that were irrelevant and insensitive." As such, she did not demonstrate a "good faith" that she was opposing a statutory violation. Her comments were insensitive enough to warrant a termination and the court said YOU CAN'T DO THAT AT WORK!

Remember, in addition to participating or opposing discrimination, an employee must also have suffered a materially adverse employment action as a result of their action(s). This can come in various forms such as termination, suspension, denial of promotion, demotion, and undeserved low ratings on job evaluations.

Lastly, to prove a retaliation claim, the employee must also prove that there was a causal connection between the protected activity and the materially adverse employment action. In other words, the employee must demonstrate that the materially adverse employment action would not have happened "but for" the protected activity. This is referred to as the causation standard.

There are various ways that an employee can prove that their protected activity was the cause of the materially adverse employment action:

1. Suspicious timing: While it may be easier to prove the causal connection if the adverse action took place shortly after the protected activity, a short period of time is not required. There have been many cases where retaliatory intent was proven even after a long period between the protected activity and adverse action.
2. Oral or written statements.
3. Comparative evidence: When another similarly situated employee who was not engaged in the protected activity was treated more favorably.
4. Inconsistent or shifting explanations: Get your story about the adverse action right!

An employer does have some defense to retaliation claims when it may appear, at face value, as if there is a causal connection. One defense may be that the employer was unaware of the protected activity. Other defenses could be that there were just simply other reasons for the adverse employment action, such as:

*   poor performance;
*   inadequate qualifications for the position sought;
*   qualifications, application, or interview performance inferior to the selectee;

- negative job references;
- misconduct (e.g., threats, insubordination, unexcused absences, employee dishonesty, abusive or threatening conduct, or theft); and
- reduction in force or other downsizing.

Not only are retaliation cases high in number, but they are high in payouts as well. Albertsons, Inc., a national grocery store chain, had to pay out 8.9 million dollars to 168 employees when they were found to have retaliated against employees who had complained of discrimination. The retaliation came in the form of denials of promotions, harder assignments, and even termination! The EEOC said YOU CAN'T DO THAT AT WORK and not only ordered Albertsons Inc. to pay monetary damages, but to provide training to employees. They would also require monitoring for four years for compliance.

Practical Considerations

Of all the claims filed at the EEOC, retaliation leads the list with 44.5% of all charges filed (and it is on the rise).

Let's explore a few reasons why and what employers can do to mitigate retaliation claims.

- One of the primary reasons for this recent surge is the expansion of the definition of what constitutes a materially adverse action by the employer. An employee previously had to demonstrate that they suffered a "tangible" adverse action, such as a termination or cut in pay; now a tangible action need not occur. A less desirable job assignment will suffice for a retaliation claim.

- Again, employers do not need to run scared from disciplining or having performance discussions with their employees because they have filed a workplace complaint, but employers must be careful to ensure that the action is warranted and not as a result of protected activity. **Keep documentation** of anything that would lead to an adverse action against an employee to cover your back!
- Middle managers are most often the sources for retaliation claims and understandably so! Middle managers manage the day-to-day operations of employees, including assigning work, performance evaluations, and discharges. As such, middle managers should be well trained on what can be considered retaliatory conduct as well as how to handle performance issues subsequent to an employee's discrimination or harassment charge.
- Employees should know how and where to report charges of harassment, discrimination and retaliation. Having an internal reporting process eases the burden of middle management and better helps an organization to provide fair and consistent outcomes.
- Be aware! Employees are more aware of their rights in the workplace. The internet has given employees access to information and guess what? They know YOU CAN'T DO THAT AT WORK!

PART VI

THE FUTURE OF YOU CAN'T DO THAT AT WORK

Chapter 16

THE FUTURE OF YOU CAN'T DO THAT AT WORK

Common mistakes managers make:

---

97. Not staying informed of recent trends and
developments in workplace law.
98. Establishing a culture based on laws and policies,
rather than civility and respect
99. Not READING or NOT OWNING a copy of this book!

Despite the vast number of federal laws that protect workers
from being mistreated, harassed, and discriminated in the
workplace, the number of employees who complain of workplace
misconduct, unlawful termination and retaliation, and being
denied workplace accommodations is growing. We're not just
talking about whiny employees either. We're talking about
employers who have either intentionally or unintentionally
discriminated against employees because of their race, gender,
national origin, religion, color, disability, age, or pregnancy status.
To prove the legitimacy of these claims, in 2016, employment
discrimination class-action settlements alone totaled 79.8
million dollars out of a total of 1.87 billion dollars of class-action

settlement payouts for workplace law violations. Again, that's just class-action settlements. Those numbers don't account for individual awards and settlements reached by regulatory agencies, amounts awarded to individuals through the federal courts, or settlements reached by employees and their employers outside the adjudication process.

Although the number of harassment, discrimination, and retaliation claims continues to increase year over year, despite organizations continuing to implement policies, processes, education, and trainings about unlawful conduct in the workplace, the American workplace has still not learned what YOU CAN'T DO AT WORK! How does this continue to happen? It boils down to culture, systems, and the systemic environment that forms a dark cloud over the American workplace.

If not at the federal level, or at the state level, workplace laws will continue to expand and multiply. Laws will continue to become more and more unclear, and employees will become more and more informed, which will cause more and more disruption in the workplace. To add to the complexity, President Trump has campaigned on a platform of creating more blue-collar jobs while also advocating for the deregulation of the workplace. As we learned from the now enjoined overtime rule, workplace law can be unpredictable, causing complete chaos for employers and employees alike. Depending on who occupies the Oval Office, Congress, and the Supreme Court of the United States, the rights that employees enjoy in the workplace can either be expanded to provide more protection or interpreted in a way that can completely change the way that they currently applied. Workplaces have to be proactive for what's next rather than being caught off guard, as was the case with the overtime rule. To do this, one must monitor state legislation and regulatory requirements, and presidential and congressional elections.

As such, here are some potential items that employers should follow that may impact workplaces on a federal level.

Proposed Federal Overtime. At the writing of this book, it is highly unlikely that the proposed federal overtime rules will go into effect in the near future. However, some states, such as New York, have already passed similar legislation with increasing salary minimums to qualify for an exemption. It is likely that many more states will follow suit as employees and labor activists are demanding more wages for employees. Without minimum wage hikes, increasing the minimum salary is another avenue for providing better salaries for workers.

Pay Equity and Transparency. The EEOC is taking a more active role in ensuring that organizations' pay practices are fair and equitable. They will be accomplishing this by requiring all private employers who are subject to Title VII jurisdiction with 100 or more employees to report pay, race, and gender details to them annually. The EEOC will make this information available to the public and will utilize the data to initiate investigations into systemic pay disparity. This federal initiative, coupled with the fact that there are over 20 states with passed and proposed pay transparency laws, ensures that equal pay will be a hot topic for a time to come.

Protections for Sexual Orientation and Gender Identity. Again, with our current presidential administration, it is highly unlikely that sexual orientation and gender identity will become explicitly protected under Title VII of the Civil Rights

Act of 1964. However, more and more states will likely include sexual orientation and gender identity as a protected class in their state civil rights legislation. Additionally, the EEOC will aggressively pursue organizations for sexual orientation and gender identity discrimination as sex-based.

Other Protected Classes. While I don't anticipate that there will be any additional protected classes under federal discrimination laws, there are a few protected classes that are increasingly making their way into state discrimination laws in addition to sexual orientation and gender identity. They are: marital status, parental status, political affiliation, credit score, criminal background, and victims of domestic violence. Municipalities seem to be moving at a faster pace at passing workplace laws than state and federal agencies. Employers and employees alike should continue to monitor all three to understand workplace protections.

Social Media. Social media isn't going anywhere, and as stated a couple of times already in this book, employees already have some significant protections regarding their use of social media. Remember, employees can discuss their terms and conditions of employment with other employees on social media and that can be considered protected concerted activity. And our achy-foot nurse who was taking selfies on the beach while on FMLA? Was she possibly protected? What I did not discuss was the ability of an employee to claim discrimination before they even meet one person from an organization. Let me explain. When an employee submits an employment application or resume, an employer usually has no idea what race, color, age, nationality, color, religion, and sometimes gender that the employee is before considering them for the next step in the hiring process. But if a hiring manager decides to take a look at their social media profile then, BOOM, many of those protected characteristics can be revealed. An employee can then say that the organization used that information in their hiring decision. It is probably a long shot to prove, but going through the headache of disproving them can be excruciating. In addition to being subjected to discrimination claims, I recommend never relying on social media as a tool to screen a candidate for many reasons. For one, how do you know you have the right person? Two, social media is not 100% reflective of a person's character. (Even if they have a drink in their hand in every photo, does that mean they won't make a good employee?) And finally, three, hiring decisions should be made on purely objective criteria. Employers should be able to determine if your candidate is a good fit by their resume, a robust interview process, background checks, and recommendations.

Paid Sick Leave and Extended Parental Leave Laws. As discussed in this book, under federal law, eligible employees working for eligible employers are entitled to 12 weeks of unpaid, job-protected leave due to their own or an immediate family member's serious medical condition, or due to the birth or placement of a child. However, as discussed, the key word is *unpaid*. Many employees do not take advantage of the protections afforded to them due to not being able to afford to lose their salaries and wages during this time. More and more states and municipalities are recognizing this and have passed paid sick time legislation. On the federal level, Donald Trump, as well as his daughter, Ivanka Trump, spoke about paid maternity leave legislation. While this would definitely be a step in the right direction, based on what we've heard about so far it would exclude fathers, parents who are adopting, and potentially, single mothers.

Medical Marijuana. To date, there is no federal law that legalizes the use medical marijuana, but state legislation is sweeping the country. Some states strictly prohibit employers from discriminating against medical marijuana cardholders, while other states say that employers do not have to accommodate marijuana use under the ADA, and the rest provide explicit protections to employees who use marijuana for medical purposes. What these laws don't protect is the ability for an employee to work while impaired. Unless an organization is located in a state with protections for medical marijuana (which are few) it is safe for most organizations to continue to have a "zero tolerance" policy for drug use in the workplace. However, the use of medical marijuana is continuing to develop, and although it is not anticipated that any protections for the use of it will be passed at the federal level, employers should keep an eye on this issue for future developments.

Joint Employment. The EEOC, the IRS, and DOL are all determined to continue to scrutinize employers who are hiring contingent workforces to possibly avoid legal liability and will continue to slowly expand the definition of *joint employer* to give workers, regardless of their classification, "access to courts" as the EEOC has defined it. To avoid being determined a joint employer, organizations can carefully define the scope of work so that the contingency worker can work as independently as possible without much direction or control and hire them on a project-by-project basis.

Labor Unions. The presence of labor unions in the workplace is continuing to decline. This is attributed to many factors, including the passage of the many laws that we have discussed in this book, the increasing credibility of human resources departments in the workplace, and the increased focus on employment engagement and satisfaction. Some have also credited the decline of labor unions to "right to work" laws. Right to work laws allow employees the benefits of union representation without having to pay union dues. Union leaders argue that right to work laws impact their power, credibility, and ability to organize. President Trump campaigned that he would bring more "blue-collar" jobs back to America. That could potentially mean that there would be more jobs created that are typically unionized. Additionally, President Trump will have the opportunity to appoint two new members to the National Labor Relations Board in the coming year, which will give him the opportunity to shape the landscape of labor relations in the United States and potentially eliminate quickie elections, which will be a relief to organizations.

A Workplace with No Policies. A slower growing trend is the gradual elimination of workplace policies. Netflix is a perfect example of a high-performing organization that operates with minimum policies. They believe in a culture of "creativity and self-discipline, freedom and responsibility." While they believe some policies are necessary, such as intolerance for harassment, dishonesty, and "preventing irrevocable disaster," they do not have vacation, dress code, or expense and travel policies. Netflix has attributed the success of this model to hiring only "A" players. While there have been a couple of publicized lawsuits against Netflix regarding non-compete agreements and violations of the ADA (which were brought by consumers, not employees), the company has managed to steer clear of high-profile employee discrimination or wage and hour claims, unlike most companies of its size. There are many lessons learned from Netflix's culture.[44]

Although the laws and regulations found in this book may change over the years to either include or exclude more protected classes in the workplace, what essentially makes a successful workplace will not. Employees will always want to feel included regardless of the way they look, regardless of religious preference, and regardless of the way they dress. Employees of all ages will always add value to an organization. Employees will always want to be paid equitably for their worth and the contributions they make to the success of an organization. Employees will always need to take time away from work to care for themselves or their loved ones without the fear of losing their job.

Most importantly, employees will always want to be respected and treated with civility in the workplace. However, I have read through literally thousands of employment discrimination cases throughout my career, and what I see is a common theme of employees who started their careers with hopes and dreams of a bright future, growth, and a feeling of self-worth, but experienced something quite different. Instead of organizations focusing their effort on providing a healthy work environment, they instead look for ways to avoid complying with laws, ignore complaints from "lower" level employees, and create and facilitate a toxic culture. When reading through the

---

[44]   McCord, P. 2014. "How Netflix Reinvented HR." *Harvard Business Review.* https://hbr.org/2014/01/how-netflix-reinvented-hr.

responses to charges of discrimination and harassment, I am often appalled and saddened.

As I stated earlier, there are over 25 laws that essentially prohibit workplace disparities of many kinds. If you think back to where we were just 100 years ago, the creation and evolution of workplace law is incredible. Yet, we have so far to go. Think about it:

- There is still uncertainty as to whether or not an organization can discriminate against someone due to their sexual orientation.
- Despite the diversity of nationalities living and working in the United States, organizations still have policies where employees are required to speak English only.
- 1 in 4 women report that they have been sexually harassed in the workplace.
- 70 percent of individuals who experience harassment never report it due to fear of retaliation.
- There are no federally mandated paid leaves, sick time, holidays, or vacations.
- Most claims filed with the EEOC are claims of retaliation.
- There is still a huge wage disparity between genders.
- Employees are sometimes not being paid at all for time worked.
- Employees are still unionizing to address unsatisfactory terms and conditions of employment.
- 28% of employees report being bullied at work.

- Over 89,000 individual claims of harassment and discrimination were filed with the EEOC in 2015.

Most of the 100 "mistakes that managers make" described in this book are mistakes that could have been avoided absent any federal legislation. Too many organizations treat their employees like political rivals. The culture of our political landscape is not about if an act was good or bad, we judge the act based on WHO did it, and if the perpetrator is on our side. If the perpetrator is on our side, we invent excuses to justify the actions. If the perpetrator is not on our side, we invent reasons to be outraged. Moreover, instead of talking to each other to gain knowledge and a better understanding of each other's concerns, we close our ears and focus on protecting the people on our team even when they're wrong. This culture may be okay for political rivals but this is NOT the way to run an organization. Organizations must not sacrifice their values to protect high-value employees. High-value employees are not limited to those who rake in large amounts of money for organizations; high-value employees are also those who are near and dear to the leadership.

Let's reflect back on Jerry Sandusky and the disgusting child rape debacle at Penn State University. Although Jerry Sandusky had not coached for a number of years and did not contribute any athletic or monetary value to the football program, he was near and dear to the leadership. And, because of the high-value status he had with the organization, he was able to have full access to football facilities even after he had been reported for sexual assaults on minors. Again, the employees are not political rivals, they are team members, and no high-value employee is worth sacrificing the reputation of the organization. Protecting high-value employees can not only cost your organization millions of dollars and much embarrassment, but protecting them can also end the careers of innocent people who are associated. Think about Joe Paterno, the legendary head football coach at Penn State. Although he had an extremely long coaching career, he was forced to retire because of the actions of someone else: Jerry Sandusky. CYOA... I would always laugh when I'd hear my husband tell his students, "I don't need YOUR help to get ME in trouble because I can do that on my own." Don't allow yourself to be in situation where a high-value employee can cause the demise of your career.

We've discussed 100 common mistakes made by leaders in the workplace. Many managers break workplace laws due to ignorance and a lack of training while other leaders may look for ways to manipulate workplace laws to cover bad behavior. Moreover, regardless of how well versed your organization is with workplace law, the most important thing to know is the Law of Civility. The culture of civility can do wonders for your organization. You may not be well-versed in labor and employment law, but you can avoid many of the mistakes listed in this book just from being nice and considerate of the needs of your employees. As a leader, you may not be familiar with the Family Medical Leave Act, but you don't need to go to law school to learn how to be sensitive to the needs of an employee who has a kid who has been diagnosed with cancer. You may not be familiar with the statutes that prohibit sexual harassment, but you don't need to pay out millions of dollars in legal fees and lawsuits to learn that you shouldn't talk about or do inappropriate and obscene sexual acts in the workplace. Employees don't expect their leaders to perfect, but they do expect for them to civil, fair, and responsive to the concerns they bring to your attention without the fear of facing retaliation. Responding to concerns, making minor adjustments, and saying "I'm sorry" can go a long way. Happy employees are the best employees.

The culture of civility will fill in the gaps where workplace laws don't do enough or are nonexistent. Dr. Martin Luther King, Jr. famously implied in his *Letters from Birmingham Jail* that all laws are not just. I want to expand on this philosophy to say that in some cases, as is described in this book, the absence of laws can be unjust as well. Just because the right thing to do isn't written on paper doesn't mean that there is a not a moral obligation attached to it. Many organizations boast integrity as a core value. Integrity is often defined as doing the right thing even when no one is watching. The underlying theme of workplace law is equality – being treated equally in the same set of conditions. When I think of equality, I again think of Dr. King, who ironically died while advocating for equal pay and working conditions for sanitation workers in Memphis, Tennessee. Unfortunately, we are still writing about many of the same issues over 50 years later. King believed that when you have equality, you have justice, but made clear the distinction between "a negative peace, which is the absence of tension, [and] a positive peace, which is the presence of justice."[45] Does your organization have positive peace or the presence of justice? Or does your organization lead by fear, retaliate against the outspoken, and/or reward "high-value" employees with unacceptable behaviors? If the answer to these two questions is "yes," well, YOU CAN'T DO THAT AT WORK. I end this book, with this quote: "injustice anywhere is a threat to justice everywhere." An organization that allows injustice to occur anywhere, by anyone, is the 100th and final mistake that absolutely should not be made in the workplace.

---

[45]   King, Martin Luther, Jr. 1994. *Letter from the Birmingham Jail*. San Francisco: Harper San Francisco.

About the Author

Natasha Bowman JD, SPHR has been leading organizations through the complex, fast-changing human resources landscape for over ten years. She has developed a reputation as an expert consultant and thought leader for organizations like The Heritage Foundation, Knowledge International, and Wiley Publishing and many others. Her expertise spans human resources management, talent management, employment law, organizational development, sourcing and recruiting, collective bargaining, and ethics and compliance. Because of her ability to diagnose workplace issues and provide proven solutions to organizations, she is often referred to as The Workplace Doctor.

Apart from rich expertise and cross-sector experience, she brings an ardent intellectual commitment to the field. Her law degree has equipped her to guide million-person companies through HR crises by designing policies, training company leaders, directing investigations and keeping the pulse of emerging trends in employment and labor law.

She is an Associate Professor at the Jack Welch Management Institute and Manhattan College and formerly sat on the faculty of Georgetown University and Fordham University. She is an international professional speaker speaking frequently for nationally recognized professional associations such the Society for Human Resources Management (SHRM), the Association for Talent Development (ATD), and Business Law Resources (BLR). She has been quoted by Bloomberg BNA, Business Insider, Fast Company, and Glassdoor.com.

Special Acknowledgments

L.K. Bennett U.S.
Anne Fontaine
Michael Benabib- Executive Photos, NYC
KGB